30 Trees

30 Trees

nd Why Landscape Architects Love Them

dited by
on Henderson

Birkhäuser
Basel

Table of Contents

And the day came when the risk to remain tight in a bud
was more painful than the risk it took to blossom.

Elizabeth Appell

Designing with Trees

30 Trees

As Paradise *(though of* God's *own* Planting*) was no longer* Paradise *then the* Man *was put into it,* to dress it, and to keep it*; so, nor will our* Gardens ... *remain long in their* perfection, *unless they are also continually* cultivated.

John Evelyn

The British savant John Evelyn (1620–1706), who is something of a patron saint for those who work in the planter's arts, demonstrated early devotion to the pleasures and benefits of planting as a young man. Rather from the start, his enthusiasm was tempered by a refined scientific eye observing the lamentable political and industrial ways of his countrymen. The wholesale destruction of forested lands to produce timber for shipbuilding in the English Civil Wars of 1642–51 alarmed him greatly, and he warned that without proper forestry practices, the Royal Navy itself, the backbone of the nation's defense, was at risk, in the most unsteady of times. His 1661 pamphlet *Fumifugium* addressed the problem of London's disastrously smoky, sooty air. It was an urgent call directly to the newly crowned king, Charles II, to rescue the promise of decent urban living for the masses from the perils of airborne pollution—just one of the treacherous maladies of life in seventeenth-century London.

In his 1664 *Sylva, or a Discourse of Forest-Trees, and the Propagation of Timber in His Majesties Dominions*, Evelyn implored Britons to stave off the loss of the forest by planting fields of trees in great numbers, and to improve the air by burning aromatic woods instead of the gravely impure sea coal that London relied on for industry and winter heat. In doing so, he drew a radical policy implication: that the relationship between trees and the properties of air—and, assuredly, between trees and human health—requires state action.

Evelyn foresaw what we now acknowledge as the Anthropocene—during which human activities have wrought consequential change to the earth's surface, its atmosphere and weather, and its more-than-human populations. For our interest, among several of his compelling urban-planning propositions, Evelyn's plans for forestry practice—a *restoration* of trees—paralleled the restoration of the divinely ordained Stuart monarchy to the crown, which he fervently hoped would improve the picture. Neither restoration endured for long. The Stuarts fell within thirty years, and London's sick air got much worse for several hundred.

Evelyn was not the first to urge planting as compensatory debt for ruination, or as pleasure. We all know of biblical figures, ancient Buddhists and Mughals, African kings, the Romans Pliny and Pompey, Medici cultivators, French hydraulic engineers and landscape gardeners, and the American reformists Muir, Olmsted, and Eliot. The voices speaking for the trees have been legion.

Ron Henderson wants today's landscape architects to record their own proclamations on planting because he knows that landscape architects share his own love of working with trees, and he believes that the reparative work of planting is desperately needed. Praise for the labor and the beauty of trees comes in this book in multiple ways: how to regard and imbibe the sensory and spatial qualities of plants; how to benefit from planting in great numbers; and what it means to a collection of people who plant to cultivate a devotion to specific species.

Gary Hilderbrand / Cambridge, USA

1

Yamataka Jindai-
zakura, on-site
sketch of one
of Japan's three
great cherry trees,
Ron Henderson,
2012

This book will appeal to a broad audience, but I hope that it will attract students of design. As an educator, I can observe with confidence that today's landscape architecture students and some of their teachers are enthusiastically seduced by highly specific biophysical, cultural, and ecological aspects of trees. Provenance, pollination, microbiological interactions, indigenous management practices, health benefits, relationships to ritual and custom, and "the rights of plants" have become the drivers of many studio and thesis projects in graduate school today. Unsurprisingly, some of the authors in this collection bring forward these same interests.

Among his own diverse plant loves, Henderson has devoted great effort to understanding cultural patterns of reverence for cherries in Japan and here in the United States (fig. 1). He has generously shared his knowledge of the techniques required to preserve and sustain ancient cherry trees. His drawings of cherries are legendary. Yet he also brings to this volume a close reading of the act of designing: of choosing, organizing, and planting a midcentury garden of wide repute, where the forms and orders of the single tree, pairs of trees, the line, the doubled row, the clump, the bosque, and other forms were deployed to shape a specific sequence of diverse spatial experiences of trees on a single site.

In the world Ron Henderson and I both wish to plant in, no pattern is accidental; spatiality is never divorced from cultural or ecological factors. All these come to bear on the exquisite task of devising a well-curated planting palette, refining a plan, and planting a part of the world, in numbers large or small.

Finally, this book is timely for the nonprofessional audience it will attract. Trees have gained in *standing*—allow me to credit the botanist Ned Friedman with this descriptor—in recent years in urban life and popular culture. Witness the growth in planning for urban-forest expansion in most major cities, but also the surge of popular-press bestsellers where trees are protagonists in narratives about saving the planet from climate disaster. These include the resoundingly popular *Overstory* by Richard Powers and Peter Wohlleben's assertions about trees as sentient beings in *The Hidden Life of Trees: What They Feel, How They Communicate; Discoveries from A Secret World*. Emanuele Coccia's remarkable philosophical treatise *The Life of Plants: A Metaphysics of Mixture*—in which he insists that because plants produce oxygen, they are foundational to all forms of life—has also gained immensely broad readership.

That trees have standing in our world has been widely embraced, finally. In these pages, landscape architects get to add their own evocations and acclamations for the lively and not-always-cooperative nonhuman living beings they work with every day. John Evelyn's urgings remain authoritative and of even greater import. Plant love is needed, now more than ever.

Abel Rodríguez / Colombian Amazon

10

Abel Rodríguez (Mogaje Guihu) is an indigenous Amazonian and nombrador de plantas (namer of plants). His tribe was displaced from its homeland in the headwaters of the Cahuinari River, and he knows that all knowledge is vulnerable without direct connections to the land and the plants.

Voice recordings by Abel Rodríguez were transcribed and freely translated from the Spanish by Alexis Arias Betancourt. The editor would like to thank Sandra Caicedo, Omayra Alvarado, and Andrés Moreno at Instituto de Visión.

Abel Rodriguez, *El árbol de la vida y la abundancia*, 2020, ink on Fabriano paper, 150 × 150 cm, courtesy of the artist and Instituto de Visión

Ese árbol de la vida, el que usted mira usted. Yo nunca lo vi, ni lo tuve. Ni en el sueño no lo vi, entonces, ¿cómo lo voy a hacer?

Entonces yo tuve que inventar, para que tenga todo el conocimiento, todo el pensamiento, todo el poder del hombre. El árbol es fruta comestible, tronco, hojas, ramas, todo. Según el creador de la tierra, nuestros padres y nuestros abuelos. Él era el principio y el ultimo. Él era aire, él era agua, él era candela, él era rayo, relámpago, todo lo que existe.

Entonces pues, en ese momento apareció un animalito que se llama ardilla Guara, tintín y zorro. Nadie se animó a pedir, a preguntarle. Y en eso pues un par de zorros llegaron allá al lugar donde está el árbol de la vida. Estamos muriendo de hambre, y no podemos subir. ¿Por qué no pueden subir? El caballo, la vaca, el chivo, el marrano y todos los animales muertos, sin piel y sin nada. La ardilla pues sube a comer y bajaba, todo llena, no le pasaba nada. ¿Quién podrá ir en busca de una herramienta? A ver si se puede tumbar esto. Ahí uno muestra el hacha. Y se cortó el tronco hasta que lo vence y el árbol se cae. Y el zorro empezó a tomar de todo. Cogió maraca, pina, caimo, uvas. Nadie se animó a pedir, a preguntarle, y así fue.

Es un árbol que nace verde y muere seco. Y ese árbol pues figuro a esa manera como lo pinte, así. Hasta aquí, había vida. Hasta ahí es la vida del palo, la vida del árbol. Hasta ahí me acuerdo.

That tree of life—the one you see—I never saw it, nor did I have it—even in my dreams.

So how will I draw it?

I had to invent it so it has all the knowledge, thought, and power of humankind. The tree is edible fruit, trunk, leaves, branches, everything—according to the creator of the earth, our parents, and our grandparents. It was the first and the last. It was air. It was water. It was fire. It was lightning.

It was everything that exists.

At a moment of imagining, a little Guara squirrel appeared—as did a fox. Then a few more foxes arrived at the place of the tree of life. “We’re starving and we can’t climb,” the foxes said. Why couldn’t they go up?

The horse, the cow, the goat, and the pig were all dead, without skin or anything, but the squirrel went up the tree and came down after eating its fill without anything happening to it.

“Who can look for something to see if this tree can be knocked down?” An ax was found and the trunk was cut until the tree fell. The fox began to take everything: cacao, pineapple, abiu, grapes. No one dared to ask the fox, and so it was.

This tree is born green and dies dry. I painted it like this—with life—the trunk and the tree.

As far as I remember.

Design-ing with Trees

A Feral Forest

Jamie Vanucchi and Karen Lutsky /
Ithaca and Minneapolis, USA

16

Jamie Vanucchi is an associate professor of landscape architecture at Cornell University, and Karen Lutsky is an assistant professor of landscape architecture at the University of Minnesota.

Jutting out into the waters of Lake Ontario, along the eastern edge of the Toronto shoreline, a new forest is growing. Composed of aspen stands and black locust groves nestled in lowlands and along ridges made of brick and concrete, exposed to intense energies of wind, water, industry, and people, the forest of Tommy Thompson Park is not old, or tall, or grand. Rather, this forest has unique lessons to share about time and change, agency and adaptation, and the tension between design and ferality in a contemporary urban forest.

1

The word "feral," meaning "not domesticated or cultivated" (*Merriam-Webster*, n.d.) or "reverted to a wild condition following escape from captivity" (Allaby 2014), is closely tied to the role of an agency and freedom that lies just beyond control. Not quite "wild," a feral plant or animal lies in a realm proximal to the human, its identity calibrated by its association and response to human control and influence. It is rarely a "desired" attribute. It often denotes lack of control or erraticism, but it also reflects an agency determined or driven by the feral entity itself. The feral has recognizable, familiar qualities but holds elements of the unknown and uncertain. In *Feral Atlas*, Anna Tsing and her coauthors (2020) note that the word is "a descriptive characteristic of a more-than-human Anthropocene" where "a focus on feral dynamics guides researchers to an approach: investigate the relationships that stimulate ferality." Notably, the ferality of the forests of Tommy Thompson Park is "stimulated" by the relationships playing out amongst a dynamic collection of actors that one could consider an assemblage, a shapeshifting collective (Anderson and MacFarlane 2011) or cohort that is historically contingent (DeLanda 2016) and emerges in time.

The park site is "new" ground constructed in what was known in the 1800s as the marsh of Ashbridge Bay, a large wetland at the mouth of the Don River that has long been a place where the sediments of the uplands wash, mix, and

2

settle along the shoreline. Wetlands like this one are feral in their own right, notoriously difficult landscapes to control amidst the constant push and pull of shifting water levels, waves, ice, and winds. As the city of Toronto grew over the twentieth century, the Don's wetlands were smothered by waste disposal and fill and became developable bayfront land. Depositions of urban demolition rubble, subway excavation spoils of bedrock and subsoil, and dredged sands and silts by the truckful (Kehm 2020, 2) assembled substrates from the city itself, the sedimentary rock it is built upon, and the lake harbor bottom to form a new peninsula, the Leslie Street Spit, extending from the city into the bay. Because it began as a gathering of diverse substrates, silts, and seeds moved and mixed by water, the site possessed more potential for wildness than other park sites. But, as top-down urban designs plans for a new marina district and shoreline transportation were debated and disputed, a common assumption was that this "trash" landscape would lie fallow. Instead, a forest emerged and exerted surprising agency over the future of the Spit.

For the last four decades, the feral forest at Tommy Thompson Park has continuously constructed, deconstructed, and reconstructed itself—not toward some planned design, but through the action of individual trees and species which find preferred niches across environmental gradients and follow their own trajectories of change. Tree species claim ground when the conditions are right, hold it while they can, and then release it in a succession of introductions, competitions, and local extinctions. Agency continuously shifts as trees interact with and change site conditions to create or exclude habitats for future species, giving rise to a dynamic patchwork of nested assemblages, each with distinct qualities.

A walk along the shoreline quickly finds one immersed in both old and new stands of eastern cottonwood (*Populus deltoides*) (fig. 1). This pioneer species requires bare soils and minimal root competition to germinate and survive. It was one of the first tree species to claim territory in the ditches along the road used by dump trucks to add material to the Spit, possibly when an airborne seed blew in from the nearby mainland (Kehm and del Tredici 2021, 106). Rarely planted in urban settings due to its weak wood and abundance of "messy," cotton-like seeds, eastern cottonwood only finds itself here by its own agency and ability to thrive in the most difficult of conditions. Political theorist Jane Bennett's definition of an assemblage, summed up by Colin McFarlane (2009, 562) as "an uneven topography of trajectories that cross or engage each other to different extents over time," fits just right with the successive waves of colonizations that introduced quaking aspen, hawthorn, staghorn sumac, and redtwig dogwood to the site. By 1991, species listed as invasive such as Russian olive and Norway maple were found alongside natives Manitoba and silver maple, less-feared exotics like white willow, and even heart-leaved willow and other species considered regionally rare (Higgins et al. 1992, 17).

A common trait among the site's vegetation is rhizomatic growth, which allows many species to survive in extreme conditions. Such growth habits, hidden just below the surface, can quickly turn a tree into a clonal grove or a shrub into a thicket. In one particular forest assemblage, three clonal forms share ground: quaking aspen, horsetail, and redtwig dogwood (fig. 2). For visitors, a striking forest experience is created by a carpet of upright green stems broken by patches of bright red and an even rhythm of light gray trunks flecked in black (fig. 3). Despite its agency to captivate, this grouping is unlikely to ever be found in traditional landscape designs, due in part to the designation of horsetail as one of "the world's worst weeds" (Holm et al. 1991, 262). However, the powerful material and expressive qualities of feral forest assemblages at this park are a key reason citizens organized themselves as "Friends of the Spit" to acknowledge the agency of nature and defend it against plans that might deny, suppress, or eradicate it.

Why does this feral forest resonate so strongly with visitors to the park? Is it

3

the unique minglings of species we might not use together, if at all? Is it the sense of fragility and wildness all at once, including forced exposure to the cycles of growth and death? Is it that this forest embodies resilience in the face of difficult and even extreme anthropocentric conditions? Regardless, the values found in this landscape have led to a design and management strategy that tends to be more responsive than directive.

Over the last few decades, the relationship between forest and landscape designers and managers at the park has been fairly gentle, and often indirect, in the form of staging conditions for diverse species combinations and small areas of planting for diversity and habitat. For example, landscape architect William Kehm, who worked on the project, notes that regrading the slopes of the confined disposal areas (cells constructed to contain dredge) invited vegetation to grow and species to populate and access the water. Likewise, access for recreation is secondary to habitat, so that the existing road is utilized for biking rather than paving other paths, allowing walking paths to "emerge" and meander. Dogs and loud, disruptive sports are not allowed (Kehm 2020, 88–89).

Using topographical shifts to create diversity in water flow, wind patterns, and experience—and allowing paths to develop in time—have permitted adaptations and interplay of shifting plant communities, habitat, and usage over the years. While there are management principles that have guided decisions, the tension between the love that grows for a particular landscape or species and the dynamism of these feral forests is likely to remain. For example, the relatively recent colonization of the park by another pioneer tree species, black locust (*Robinia pseudoacacia*), is currently testing design restraint. Because black locusts have the capacity to fix nitrogen across fast-growing colonies, they will begin to reshape the forest toward species that prefer fertile soils. While some management has been done to try to control these stands, hopefully the acknowledgment of the forest's own agency will keep such moves in check. If this feral forest has taught us anything, it is that delight and surprise can be born from such transformation, and that relinquishing some control and embracing change might allow us to be better participants in the new forest assemblage.

Allaby, M. 2014. *A Dictionary of Zoology*, 4th ed. Oxford: Oxford University Press. https://www.oxfordreference.com/viewbydoi/10.1093/acref/9780199684274.013.3251.

Anderson, B., and C. McFarlane. 2011. "Thinking with Assemblage." *Area* 43, no. 2 (June): 124–27.

Bennett, J. 2010. *Vibrant Matter: A Political Ecology of Things*. Durham: Duke University Press.

DeLanda, M. 2016. *Assemblage Theory*. Edinburgh: Edinburgh University Press.

Higgins, V., S. Denzel, and N. Fazari. 1992. *Plant Communities of the Leslie Street Spit: A Beginner's Guide*. Toronto: Friends of the Spit and the Botany Conservation Group, Department of Botany, University of Toronto.

Holm, L. G., Plucknett, D. L., Pancho, J. V., and Herberger, J. R. 1991. *The World's Worst Weeds: Distribution and Biology*. Malabar, FL: Krieger.

Kehm, W. H. 2020. *Accidental Wilderness: The Origins and Ecology of Toronto's Tommy Thompson Park*. Toronto: Aevo UTP.

Kehm, W. H., and P. del Tredici. 2021. "From Rubble to Refuge: Tommy Thompson Park in Toronto, Canada." *Landscape Architecture Frontiers* 9, no. 1: 104–11.

McFarlane, C. 2009. "Translocal Assemblages: Space, Power and Social Movements." *Geoforum* 40, no. 4 (July): 561–67.

Merriam-Webster. n.d. "Feral (*adj*.)." Accessed June 6, 2023. https://www.merriam-webster.com/dictionary/feral.

Tsing, A. L., J. Deger, A. Keleman, and F. Zhou. 2020. "Introduction to Feral Atlas." In *Feral Atlas: The More-Than-Human Anthropocene*, edited by A. L. Tsing, J. Deger, A. Keleman, and F. Zhou. Stanford: Stanford University Press. https://feralatlas.supdigital.org/index?text=introduction-to-feral-atlas&ttype=essay&cd=true.

Clumps—Compact Places over Time

Roland Gustavsson / Alnarp, Sweden

22

Roland Gustavsson is a landscape architect, researcher, and teacher. He is a professor of planting design and landscape management at the Swedish University of Agricultural Sciences' Department of Landscape Planning, where he founded the Alnarp Landscape Laboratory.

The bridge between urban and rural landscapes. I argue for enlarging our mental set of reference landscapes. As a landscape architect I have never felt embarrassed to one day be in an ancient woodland in southern Sweden and the next day in central London, Amsterdam, or the Hague. Obviously I have found it rewarding to bridge urban and rural systems; it brings a freshness, a greater differentiation, and an ability to go into depth. An expanded urban world risks losing a deeper insight about systems of nature and older cultural systems that depend on manual cultivation. It becomes easy to become alienated from productive landscapes when we don't have them around us every day. To illustrate the importance of expanding our references, I have chosen forms and elements here that belong to grazed landscapes with trees, including coppice systems.

Trees are connected to forest systems as high-forest types with a closed canopy, but they also have a key role in more open systems in which you encounter trees as isolated individuals, in clumps, and in groups. First, there are low-forest systems, dependent on regular coppicing, for which there are few living references around us today. Second, there is the biologically and morphologically diverse semi-open grazed landscape, varying between clumps, open-grown trees, and trees with one trunk, two trunks, five trunks, ten trunks, and more. If the English landscape park as a style invites criticism for being oversimplified and too standardized, there may be good reasons to reevaluate the originals, which were designed with variation and differentiation in mind. Third, there is the wooded meadow mosaic (a mixed landscape type), which often contains both the closed parts and the open parts—and endlessly variable combinations.

The compact clump. In the vocabulary of the legendary English landscape architect Capability Brown (1716–83), this specific kind of mixed type falls into categories described as "dots, belts and clumps" (Braae 2023, 24). Inside a clump, trees create mass with more edges, a subtype of clump one might call a "clump of compactness." As a subtype it is distinct due to its enormous density of trunks. It could also be argued that there is a similarity to the coppice type, with its shrub-tree form, and both could start in the same way. However, there is a difference between the compact clump and the coppice. A coppice demands management and harvesting; the tree species never become treelike. The compact clump is free-growing and develops its own natural pattern. Clumps measuring about 3–5 m in diameter, in which the trees live with their neighbors in a state of codominance, leads to layering and competition—not species suppression. Dense planting of the clump, at a spacing of about 30 × 30 cm between plants, supports codominance.

This landscape type has its origin in the rural cultivated landscape, in semi-open grazed landscapes and wooded meadows. It is found as mosaic vegetation types across Europe—from Scandinavia to Portugal and from Ireland to the Baltic countries.

A biological system. By growing in compact clumps, the trees protect each other. Those along the edges are browsed by animals and exposed to frost and desiccation, but those inside the clump are protected. European hornbeam (*Carpinus betulus*) is a preferred species due to its ability to withstand heavy grazing and browsing. Other species common in coppice systems are also effective: beech, oak, wild cherry, pear, plum, hazel, bird cherry, linden, alder, and willow. Some of these can grow by clones and suckers in systems where the mother tree supports the offspring. In England, it has been found that hazel coppices can grow to be over seven hundred years old (Peterken and Jones 1989).

Bäckasjögärde, Sweden and Mers-sur-Indre, France: Origins of the Clump as Living Landscape

Bäckasjögärde is located in one of the richest regions of grazed open woodlands in the world's temperate climate zone. I have found similar highly differentiated, high-quality "clump" landscapes in Romania, Serbia, central France, and northern Portugal. The example of Bäckasjögärde has been used to gain a deeper understanding of the clump as a vegetation type, and it has also been used as a model in several design projects and contexts in Sweden, Denmark, and England (Tregay and Gustavsson 1983, 71–73, 89, 92; Busse Nielsen et al. 2023, 172, 173, 176).

The original example of the clump as a living landscape is from the 1970s (fig. 1). When measured on February 26, 2023, it had grown to a diameter of 3.5 m and a crown width of 17 m when measured on February 26, 2023 (fig. 2). It consists of thirty-four trunks when counted 1 m above the base; thirty-two hornbeams and two oaks. This means fewer individuals are found near the ground, since trunks have merged over the years as they stabilized against the wind. This clump began with a ring of stones that protected the very small trees from grazing.

Mers-sur-Indre, in France, reminds us that we should commit to patience so we can experience how beautiful trees can be if they are allowed to get old. This profile diagram, by Linn Gustavsson from 2010, reflects the strong character of an ancient coppice (fig. 3).

1

Four Designed Landscapes with Clumps

Oakwood. Robert Tregay's design for a greenbelt near homes and gardens in Oakwood, Warrington New Town, England, was inspired by the grazed Scandinavian landscape at Bäckasjögärde. The project achieved biodiversity through design and natural development by remodeling the landform of the site to create moisture gradients. In the 1983 project report, the signature cluster plantings are described

2

as “individual transplants in meadows” (Tregay and Gustavsson 1983, 71) (figs. 4 and 5). Oakwood received an award for landscape restoration in 1981 and another for best housing for new towns in 1983. More recently, Tregay made the leap to a “dense planted clump” using hornbeam on his private estate in England.

Backsippan Children’s Forest. A young birch forest (in bright green in the northwest corner of the map) was bought by the town of Ronneby, Sweden, to serve Backsippan, a children’s day-care center (fig. 6). The forest was initially thinned and complemented by dense planting of 5 m circles of hornbeam, beech, linden, hazel, rowan, spruce, and pine. Three circles with open centers were planted around the perimeter of the project. My plan from 2014 evolved into the 2019 plan, which shows the growth of the plants and the network of paths and rooms that were laid out together with the children, who used wheelbarrows and two heaps of sand in each corner of the forest to start making their own spaces (fig. 7). The dense, compact plantings, such as the beech circle, invite adventure play (mini paths, mini rooms, and material explorations) while maintaining healthy plants in and around the circles.

Revisiting the Children’s Forest (which received international recognition for its “cradle-to-cradle” model of material reuse/recycling and its invention of the “children’s mini forest”) on May 10, 2023, affirmed that these densely planted circles, now 5 m in diameter, have thrived despite intensive use by the children because the plant density successfully protects the trees (fig. 8).

Other observations include that the area nearest the daycare has become too intensely managed; pockets of wilderness are needed. The double hornbeam hedge has grown to the height of the children and is making promising progress, with established inner rooms tall enough to

3

4

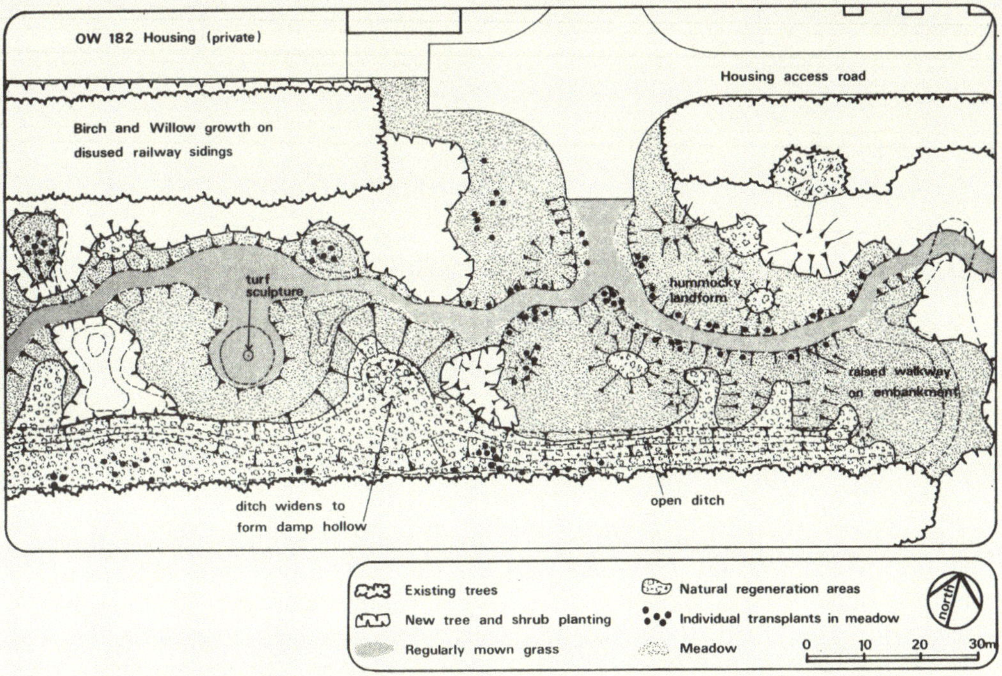

Figure 47. Diversity through design and natural development. Remodelling the landform of the site shown in figure 46 will create moisture gradients and lead to variety in vegetation. *Variation genom gestaltning och naturlig utveckling. Ommodellering av landformer i området som visades i figur 46. En fuktighetsgradient och en bas för variation i växtligheten tillskapas härmed.*

5

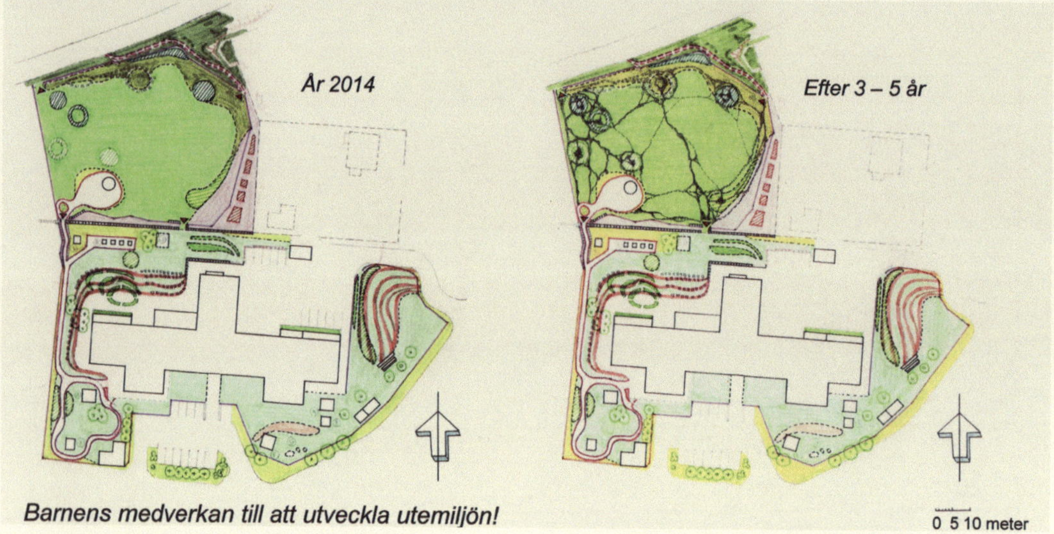

6

cast shadows (fig. 9). In the 100 × 100 m birch forest, which had been carefully thinned, the understory circles have established an order in the forest for the rooms and networks created by the children (fig. 10). For them it is a pretty large forest. The circles, some of hazel, have not yet become teenagers but are substantial enough to stimulate the children. A compact beech clump, eight years old and already containing micro paths and rooms, might look insubstantial, but for the children it is a distinct island in the structure of the forest. A compact planting of spruce 15 m in diameter—similar in size to the other circles—has an access opening and has lost some plants in the middle but offers enough space for the children to mark the place with a collection of branches and stumps without damaging the other spruces (fig. 11).

Filborna Nature Park. I designed Filborna Nature Park in Helsingborg, Sweden, in the 1980s with clumps of hornbeam, linden, wild cherry, aspen, birch, and beech. The clumps are a signature feature of the park. Filborna is the main recreation area for the eastern part of the city, and the clumps are an experiment, especially with regard to the design of their edges.

Sletten Landscape Laboratory. Sletten Landscape Laboratory, which I designed, was constructed in Holstebro, Denmark, in 2006 and has received two national awards. The compact oak clumps will have to slow down and gain their personality through competition with the meadow plants from the housing project's more extensive plantings.

Concluding remarks. The hornbeam clump, in all its distinctiveness and compactness, illustrates a form that appears

7

8

9
10

11

to be important for future designed landscapes. As a type, it is easily overlooked due to its similarity to the "normal" clump so often found in classic English landscape parks, but by looking at living references found in the rural landscape, such as the grazed open woodland systems of Bäckasjögärde and the old coppices of Mers-sur-Indre, we gain a fuller understanding, expand our possibilities, and discover compact clumps such as those described above.

Braae, E. M. 2023. "Plant Blindness." *Landskab* 2 (April): 23–25.

Busse Nielsen, A., L. Diedrich, and C. Szanto, eds. 2023. *Woods Go Urban: Landscape Laboratories in Scandinavia*. Wageningen: Blouwdruk.

Peterken, G. F. and E. W. Jones. 1989. "Forty Years of Change in Lady Park Wood: The Young-Growth Stands." *Journal of Ecology* 77, no. 2 (June): 401–29.

Tregay, R., and R. Gustavsson. 1983. *Oakwood's New Landscape: Designing for Nature in the Residential Environment*. Alnarp: Sveriges Lantbruksuniversitet.

One Tree, Row, Two Trees, Allée, Grid, Hedge, Clump, Woods

Ron Henderson / Chicago, USA

30

Ron Henderson is a professor in the Landscape Architecture + Urbanism program at the Illinois Institute of Technology and founding principal of LIRIO Landscape Architecture.

The disposition of trees establishes fundamental spatial, material, and temporal structures for gardens and landscapes. Designing with identifiable orders, or tree planting types, provides frameworks for shaping space, orchestrating experience, influencing plant growth, and enhancing ecological performance, among other functions. As the French theorist Quatremère de Quincy (1755–1849) wrote in the *Encyclopédie méthodique*, "the word 'type' presents less the image of a thing to copy or imitate completely than the idea of an element which ought itself to serve as a rule for the model" (Younés 1999, 254). Consequently, "this law or abstract principle that guides any artistic production is therefore eternal and ideal, although the models that arise from the application of these principles are infinite in its variations" (Lee 2011).

It is the infinite variations that emerge from seemingly simple planting types that distinguish each landscape. A specimen camphor tree is very different from a specimen lacebark pine. An allée of live oaks is very different from an allée of plane trees. An allée of lindens spaced at 5 m on center is very different from one planted at 12 m on center. Clumps designed by Capability Brown (1716–83) are different from clumps designed by Roland Gustavsson. Species selection, tree spacing, and contexts matter.

To explore these orders, it is illustrative to consider the Miller Garden in Columbus, Indiana, designed by Dan Kiley—a garden that exemplifies the

1

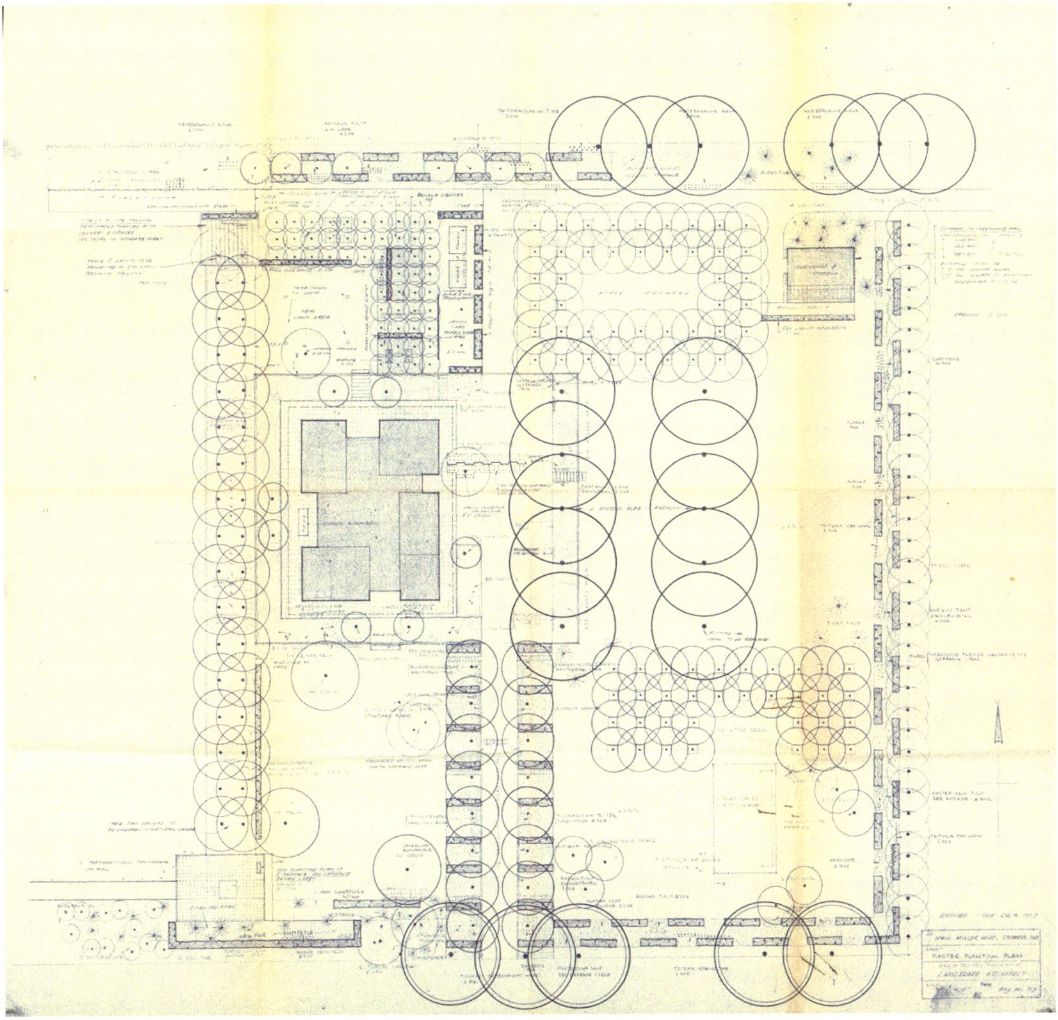

manner in which gardens can be structured with tree planting types. Recounting his experience of European landscapes following his deployment as designer of the courtroom for the Nuremberg Trials, Kiley wrote, "I wondered—I may have shouted—'Why didn't anyone ever tell me?' I was eager to apply this rich vocabulary of allée, bosque, boulevard, and *tapis vert* and to explore its potential within the modern environment" (Kiley and Amidon 1999, 18). The plan of the 5.26 ha Miller Garden documents the way Kiley used these and other tree planting types inspired by travels in Europe to structure the garden (fig. 1).

One tree: European beech and saucer magnolia. A pendulous European beech (*Fagus sylvatica*) stands sentinel at the front door of the Miller House. As the beech has matured over the past seventy years, it has lifted its limber branches to drape across the entry court in such a way that one must negotiate this veil of branches as one walks to the recessed front door (fig. 2).

This beech shares command of the entry court with another singular tree, a saucer magnolia (*Magnolia ×soulangeana*), establishing two iconic and focal specimen trees at the entrance to the house. This is an arrival tree, a welcoming tree whose early flowering is a spirit-lifting encounter. The original magnolia was damaged by a storm in 2023 and has been replaced by another of the same kind.

Row: White oaks, red maples, and sycamores (now also red maples). Two parallel rows—each containing five white oaks (*Quercus alba*)—are planted just far enough apart that they are legible as rows rather than an allée. These oaks anchor the house to the upper garden and are among the few trees from Kiley's initial planting that remain (fig. 3).

A line of red maples (*Acer rubrum*) are planted along Washington Street between the public street and the staggered hedge of arborvitae that is the public face of the property. Another row of red maples "trim out" the south side of the expansive lawn, where they geometrically clarify the edge of the property and establish an experiential sequence that connects the upper garden to the Flatrock River. A shallow flight of steps descends from the southern terminus of the honey locust allée and leads to a trodden path that slips just behind the maples. Like the honey locust allée, it is a single row of trees that precisely separate where one walks from the topography of the vast lawn. This row of maples was originally planted as three rows of sycamores (*Platanus* sp.), which did not thrive. The new species and spatial structure are clearly much different, but the primary garden-making strategy—to define the south edge of the lawn—is consistent in both design resolutions (fig. 4).

Two trees: European beeches and saucer magnolias. Both the east (front) and west doors are marked by European beech trees. While a singular specimen flanks the front door, a pair of them frame the west door that leads from the sunken living room pit to the honey locust allée and the lawn beyond. The high canopy of this pair is visible as one passes under the front-door beech, as a hint at the relationship among species and procession through the house and garden.

While one magnolia stands at the entry court, pairs of saucer magnolia stand at each side of the south (family area) and north (dining area) doors. Trees in pairs establish gates or thresholds to pass between. Their pairing establishes parallax, where their relationship to each other changes dynamically as observers change position relative to the pair. In habit, two trees may merge canopies or may exhibit crown shyness, where the lateral branches of adjacent trees refuse to intermingle. In cases where environmental factors, such as wind, influence tree habit, two tree canopies can merge into characteristic airfoil shapes. At the Miller Garden, these magnolias are spaced apart so that their canopies do not merge and they stand as paired sentinels marking these secondary doors of the house.

Allée: Horse chestnuts (now buckeyes) and honey locusts. Arrival at the property was originally through an allée

2

3

4

5

6

7

of horse chestnuts (*Aesculus hippocastanum*) which have since been replaced by the native Ohio buckeye (*Aesculus glabra*), another species in the same genus. In early spring, the large upright panicles of flowers festoon one's arrival home.

The allée of thornless honey locusts (*Gleditsia triacanthos* var. *inermis* "Moraine") along the western edge of the upper garden forms an arboreal loggia that overlooks the lawn and floodplain forest beyond and protects the house from western sun and wind. Kiley planted honey locust allées in several projects—for instance, Milton Lee Olive Park in Chicago—with varied spacing. At the Miller Garden, the thirty-six honey locusts are spaced 6.7 m on center in the north-south direction, parallel with the sloping bank, and 5.3 m in the east-west direction. Looking down the allée, the wider spacing of the trees opens the lateral and diagonal view. Describing another honey locust planting (a bosque) at the Third Block of Independence Mall in Philadelphia, Kiley states that these trees "should be closely planted for compositional effect (void to solid) which automatically increases the feeling of scale and space. ... This is one of the salient design features in the

8

contemporary landscape and reflects nature much more than wide spacing" (Kiley and Amidon 1999, 42).

Grid: Redbuds (now crabapples) and apples. Eastern redbuds (*Cercis canadensis*) were originally planted in the north garden outside the dining room and kitchen. These were replaced in 1999 with crabapples (*Malus* sp.) by the landscape architect, Jack Curtis. The landscape architect Peter Lindsay Schaudt, who worked with Kiley in the mid-1980s, once remarked that Kiley did not like crabapples because they are "too heavy, too highly textured" (Schaudt 2015). The redbud's graceful superiority of habit reminds us that species selection is a fundamental garden-making decision. For me, the redbuds are superior and should be replanted. Two orchards structure the north and south ends of the front garden. These gridded plantings—forty-two apple trees (*Malus domestica*) in the north orchard and thirty-four in the south orchard—were replanted in 2021.

Hedge: Arborvitae and yews. The perimeter of the upper garden is defined by hedges. Along Washington Street, an offset, staggered hedge of arborvitae (*Thuja* sp.) in 6 m segments was originally sheared with a narrow top and wider bottom to provide greater sun exposure for even distribution of foliage but is now sheared in a more boxy shape. The original horse chestnuts along the entry driveway were originally underplanted with arborvitae, but these were replaced with yews (*Taxus* sp.) as shade increased from the maturing trees.

Clumps: Willows and pines. The clumps of the Miller Garden are different from those described by Roland Gustavsson in his essay in this volume. Those at the Miller Garden, primarily willows, are deployed in expansive landscapes with meadows or long views such as the western lawn, where they help transition from garden to woodland. There are also clumps or stands of pines that mass along the perimeter of the property—especially at the service entry in the northeast corner and at the south end of the honey locust allée. Here, these evergreen trees establish a deep green massing, giving year-round structure to the garden.

Woods: Various trees, shrubs, and herbaceous plants. Kiley was invited to design the garden after the house was under construction—when the site was largely cleared and the upper garden established as a level plinth. However, he did inherit a woodland on the lower floodplain of the Flatrock River, where he proposed a "Romantic Garden" connected to the house by the original triple row of plane trees, which terminated at the woodland in a square terrace. Kiley's drawings show a stream inlet with many crossings and a circular space in the woodland garden's northwest corner. This was never built, although the woodland garden is now curated with a richly textured surface of spring ephemerals and drifts of redbuds.

Planting types in transition. Planting types that rely on precise spacing or order are, of course, subject to disorder when one or more of the original trees does not thrive. At the Miller Garden, this question requires critical consideration. The north garden redbuds, north and south apple orchards, honey locust allée, triple rows of sycamores edging the lawn, horse chestnut allée at the south entrance drive (including the hedges under the trees), and saucer magnolia that commanded the arrival court have all been replaced over the past sixty years. Gardens order the world, and the world reorders gardens.

Kiley, D., and J. Amidon. 1999. *Dan Kiley: The Complete Works of America's Master Landscape Architect*. Boston: Little, Brown.

Lee, C. C. M. 2011. "Type." The City as a Project. Published August 16, 2011. https://thecityasaproject.org/2011/08/type/.

Schaudt, P. 2015. "Dan Kiley and the Miller House." FASLA lecture at the Indianapolis Museum of Art, Indianapolis, USA, April 9, 2015. https://www.youtube.com/watch?v=XYV_gfUrpfo.

Younés, S. 1999. *The True, the Fictive, and the Real: The Historical Dictionary of Architecture of Quatremère de Quincy*. London: Andreas Papadakis.

Increments of Time in Japanese Cherry Blossoms

Ron Henderson and Toru Mitani /
Chicago, USA, and Tokyo, Japan

40

Ron Henderson is a professor in the Landscape Architecture + Urbanism program at the Illinois Institute of Technology and founding principal of LIRIO Landscape Architecture.

Toru Mitani leads the Landscape Lab at the University of Tokyo's Department of Architecture and is founding partner of studio on site.

Kaika, the first blossoms, are recorded at official cherry trees in cities and towns across Japan each spring. This initiates a sequence of descriptive terms that describe the blossoms as they emerge and fall to the ground. Cherry blossoms in Japan are measured in many ways: fleeting moments, hours, days, four seasons, seventy-two seasons, lifetimes, and eons (fig. 1).

A season of cherry blossom terms. After *kaika*, the buds continue to blossom, with each stage described by specific terms. Ten percent blooming is *ichibu-zaki*. Twenty percent is *nimbu-zaki*. Thirty percent is *sanbu-zaki*, and so on. *Mankai* indicates that the tree is in full bloom (figs. 2A and 2B). Another sequence of terms marks the blossoms' descent, starting with *maihajime* (when they begin to fall and scatter) and culminating with *hazakura* (when all the blossoms have fallen from the tree). *Rokubu hazakura* indicates that sixty percent of young leaves have emerged on the cherry tree—a sign that leaves are supplanting blossoms on the branches. *Shichibu hazakura* indicates that seventy percent of young leaves have emerged, and so on.

A fleeting moment of cherry blossoms: Hanafubuki. Perhaps the most anticipated of all cherry blossom events is *hanafubuki*, or "flower snowstorm," when falling petals swirl in the wind as they fall to the ground. At the Zen temple Ryōan-ji in Kyoto, a weeping cherry tree growing just outside the rammed-earth wall reaches its branches into the garden. In the summer, autumn, and winter, these branches are discreet; the renowned garden of fifteen stones arrayed on a sea of raked gravel is the focus of contemplation. However, in the spring, the tree's pink blossoms sway in the breeze to animate this space. As a storm front approached on a late spring day in 2012, the cascading, blossom-laden branches of the cherry tree began to sway. A flurry of petals swirled in the air and settled to the ground—only to disappear, as if melting, into the raked white gravel: a flower snowstorm (fig. 3).

1

Kaika (top left), *Mankai* (top right) and various phases of cherry blossoms are shown in paintings by Koha Horii in Sano, T., and K. Honda. 1961. *Sakura: Flowering Cherries of Japan*.

Eons of cherry trees: Geology and climate change. The cherry tree is often cited as having migrated from the Himalayas to Japan after the last Ice Age. In a 2012 interview with Ron Henderson, Sano Tōemon, a gardener and landscape architect whose family has cared for Kyoto's imperial cherry trees in Kyoto for sixteen generations, remarked that the *sakura* has found its home in Japan. In the course of this migration, rapid by paleobotanical standards, the genus has proven both adaptable and mobile. Cherries are also valuable for climate-change research due to the records of blossom times carefully documented in many regions of Japan for over a thousand years. Richard Primack and Hiroyoshi Higuchi (2007, 17) note that these records are widely regarded as the oldest such human record of plant phenology.

Millenia of sakura: Cultural history in one of the three great cherry trees. Venerable cherry trees are monuments to Japanese history. An Edo higan (*Prunus itosakura*) in Gifu Prefecture known as Usuzumi-zakura ("pale sumi cherry tree") was planted approximately 1,500 years ago by Emperor Keitai (d. 531), according to village records. Before his accession to the throne, Keitai—then known as Ohodo—was persecuted by Emperor Yuryaku. Ohodo sought refuge in the mountains of Mino, but when he was twenty-nine years old, he received a message that he had been named the new emperor. Before he left the village, he planted flowering cherry trees on the site where his second son, Hino Sumitakatanoo, had been born. He commemorated the event with a poem, which appears on a plaque at the park where the tree stands: "Oh! Gray cherry blossom trees I leave as my memento. Prosper the name of the tree forever." Although one tree died after planting, the other remains. The blossoms of this tree are renowned for their pale gray and muted pink color (fig. 4).

2A
2B

3

4

A day of cherry blossoms: Morning, evening, and night. *Yamazakura*, the mountain cherry (*Prunus serrulata* var. *spontanea*) is famously found in the Yoshino mountains and depicted in Kanō Isen'in Naganobu's (1577–1654) misty *Mount Yoshino Cherry Blossoms* (fig. 5). The Edo-era scholar Norinaga Motoori (1730–1801) wrote that the truest spirit of Japan is found in the *yamazakura* under the rising sun: "If we are to ask about the spirit of the Japanese, it is mountain cherry blossoms that bloom fragrantly in the morning sun" (Ohnuki-Tierney 2002, 106).

Norinaga's poem reveals the changing moods of cherry blossoms, and blossom viewers, throughout the day. The rising sun casts a glow on morning blossoms (*asazakura*), which emerge with the misty pink dew of the mountain valleys as in Hiroshige's (1797–1858) *View of Morning Cherry Blossoms in the New Yoshiwara* (fig. 6). Hiroshige also depicted evening blossoms (*yuzakura*) at fading light in his *Cherry Blossoms at Night on Nakanocho in the Yoshiwara*, where the blossoms are illuminated by lanterns and moonlight (fig. 7). Night blossoms (*yo-zakura*) are imbued with *yugen*—what the Zen master D. T. Suzuki (2010, 69) called "cloudy impenetrability."

A season of cherry blossoms: National enthusiasm and rites of youthful passage. Each spring brings a heightened awareness of the approach of the "cherry blossom front" (*sakura zensen*), with constant updates from the Japan Meteorological Society. In the ancient Japanese calendar, which has seventy-two seasons, March 26–30 is known as *sakura hajimete hiraku*, or "first cherry blossoms." The blossoms are commonly associated with the annual transitions of the Japanese school calendar, in which graduation is held in early spring. Starting in 1959, students applying to Waseda University were notified of their entrance exam results by one of two telegrams: *sakura saku* ("cherry tree blooms") if accepted, or *sakura chiru* ("petal fell") if not accepted. Such telegrams are no longer sent, of course, but the association between the cherry blossom and the season of academic transition remains. Graduations are heralded by *sakura*-themed kimonos. Classmates celebrate under the cherry trees, and new employees, fresh from the universities, are commonly assigned to secure prime spots under the cherry trees for *hanami* (cherry blossom viewing). The alignment of the bloom periods with graduation, however, is changing. The average date for *kaika* is occurring earlier—a situation attributable to climate change.

An event for cherry blossoms: The celebration of hanami. Contemporary Japanese architect Toyo Ito described *hanami* as the quintessential Japanese construction; a blanket is laid on the

ground to define areas of action and performance (fig. 8). Following the descent of the cherry blossoms, the blankets are removed—an act that signals the end of the architecture as well. The celebration of *hanami* is captured by Ito in his essay "Vortex and Current":

> The scene of a cherry-blossom viewing party, where people drink sake with friends on a red carpet under trees and paper lanterns or inside open tents, represents the fundamental character of Japanese architecture. First of all, people come together to see the cherry blossoms in full bloom, and then primitive architecture (i.e., the carpet and the tent) is built for the event. It is not that the architecture is there at the beginning; on the contrary, it is the human act of getting together that exists first. It is only afterwards that architecture comes into being to envelop the action. The party reaches its peak when, at sunset, dusk deepens, and the scene is veiled in increasing darkness. Some start singing while others dance to the music. As the night wears on, the people, getting tired of pleasure, take down the tents and go home, leaving the cherry blossoms floating in the dark-like clouds. The end of the event means the simultaneous end of the architecture as well. (Ito 1992, 22–23)

Design with cherry blossoms: Gardens of gravity and desire. The falling cherry blossoms also contribute to the history of garden design in Japan, where cherry trees are carefully sited on sloped

5

6

7

8

10

9

11

banks, along streams, at bridge crossings, and at other sites where blossoms collect on moss, streams, ponds, paths, and stones.

At Ritsurin Garden in Takamatsu, a single Edo higan has been trained to lean over a shallow crease between two small landforms amidst an extensive stand of Japanese black pines (*Pinus thunbergii*). A two-legged support has been placed to pull the cherry tree over the crease, which runs downhill toward one of the park's ponds. As petals fall, they litter the slopes of the small hills and gather in the crease—creating a cherry blossom stream. This cherry tree is the lone deciduous tree in the broad expanse of pine trees for which Ritsurin Garden is renowned. A vista across the adjacent pond reveals a wide panorama of pines with a singular pale pink mass standing out against the deep green (fig. 9).

At Kōraku-en in Okayama, near the south gate of the castle garden, a long row of Edo higans are planted high atop a sloped bank, at the base of which are a path and a small stream (fig. 10). A clipped hedge surmounting the bank emphasizes the overhead reach of the cherry branches above the path. The steep slope of the bank forms a tilted plane that collects and displays the fallen blossoms to passersby along the path. This common garden device—the tilting of the ground plane to better present the surface—is powerfully employed here, where fallen petals litter the bank. Petals also fall across the path and into the stream, which gathers them into *hana-ikada* (flower rafts) (fig. 11) that float downstream and through the garden of a tea house.

No flower falls to the earth as beautifully as the petals of the *sakura* (fig. 12).

12

Ito, T. 1992. "Vortex and Current: On Architecture as Phenomenalism." *Architectural Design* 60, no. 9–10 (September–October): 22–23.

Ohnuki-Tierney, E. 2002. *Kamikaze, Cherry Blossoms, and Nationalisms*. Chicago: University of Chicago Press.

Primack, R., and H. Higuchi. 2007. "Climate Change and Cherry Tree Blossom Festivals in Japan." *Arnoldia* 65, no. 2: 14–22.

Sano, T., and K. Honda. 1961. *Sakura: Flowering Cherries of Japan*. Kyoto: Mitsumura Suiko Shoin.

Suzuki, D. T. 2010. *Zen and Japanese Culture*. Princeton: Princeton University Press.

30 Trees

Acer macrophyllum

bigleaf maple

Maximum Green

Shannon Nichol / Seattle, USA

52

Shannon Nichol is a landscape architect who co-founded GGN in 1999.

Just as autumn foliage is celebrated in some places, my home region of the Pacific Northwest has its own seasonal spectacle. This event occurs in early summer rather than autumn, and it offers sensory immersion in a specific gradient of glowing, chartreuse-based green. The apex of this show is usually in early to mid-June. I think of this as Maximum Green Week (fig. 1).

Bigleaf maple is the glowing star of Maximum Green Week, lighting up entire valleys with its rain-fed, youthful lushness and muscularity. Its namesake leaves—the largest of any maple—have just reached their mature size, which often exceeds the 30.5 cm specified in some botanical references. When backlit, these newly emerged, translucent leaves appear to be made of Mountain Dew.

1

2

By July, they will darken and become opaque.

Bigleaf maple's pupil-flooding phytogreen is especially exciting when viewed from beneath the tree's cathedral-like branches (fig. 2). The vaulted ceilings of its glowing canopies soar impossibly high over a person crossing the anomaly of a bright stream ravine in the otherwise dark and leathery coniferous forest.

For urban and garden use, we've been told, bigleaf maple is too big, grows too joyously, clogs drains, and is short-lived. "Right tree, right place," we've been told. But this bioregion is the right place for this tree. It is on us newcomers to figure out how to successfully retain its glory—and crucial habitat value—in our built environment.

However, this tree is banned by the city of Seattle in its rights-of-way due to the "weedy" management shortcomings that come with any faster-growing species of tree that excels in quickly healing and shading the open wounds that we create.

Bigleaf maple does present a leaf-drop event that resembles many layers of soggy paper bags, and it has a less-than-classic-oak lifespan. These are the costs of its first-responder speed and its locally tuned performance. These practical management challenges are real, but they are equal to or milder than those of many exotic tree species that are permitted by most Pacific Northwest cities, which drop limbs over town and country while producing few if any biological benefits.

Depending on who does the estimating, there are only about two or three native, large, deciduous tree species on the designer's small menu in this region. And only one—bigleaf maple—happily and reliably grows into a vase-shaped, high-canopied "shade tree" with open sight-lines for humans and retail signage below. Physically, these are classically desirable trees for urban street standards, parks, and prospect-and-refuge conversations around the globe, but with the bonus of locally tuned Maximum Green powers.

3

I've therefore incorporated bigleaf maple as the primary shade tree in many of GGN's projects in this region. At the Bill & Melinda Gates Foundation, 150 bigleaf

4

5

maples were planted around the campus's central rainwater garden, in the spirit of the foundation's culture of "local roots, global mission" (fig. 3). Even some local people didn't recognize this beautiful and elegant native tree when it was included in a more crisply detailed architectural context—a setting normally reserved for exotic nursery trees in this recently colonized region.

The success of the Gates Foundation's bigleaf maples—and some lessons we've learned from failures in the sandiest-soiled rooftop planters in which we've tested it—have motivated my colleagues and me to keep iterating to develop reliable planting and management methods for incorporating bigleaf maple in urban landscapes.

This would be worth figuring out if only to sustain the species's crucial role in supporting the dwindling populations of native insects that feed so many native bird and animal species, during this sixth mass extinction.

Of course, we may now be saved from the manageable task of integrating bigleaf maple into our built environment. A recent mass die-off of this species has swept through the coastal region. Shockingly browned valleys and horribly stunted new growth first showed up in the years after a series of record-setting summer heatwaves and irregular weather.

Suppressing some terror and disbelief that this is all really happening in my short lifetime, I have reluctantly slowed down a bit in the planting of my favorite tree. I push its limits more hesitantly in heat-exposed urban conditions where I might have previously gotten away with doing so.

But I will continue to plant bigleaf maples with abandon in moist, relatively sheltered spots where they still seem to stand a reliable chance (fig. 4). I will do so to soften the curve of their decline and simply to share with others the joy of their achingly beautiful form and reassuring lushness. These trees are uniquely and radically expressive of the raw, rain-slicked, and big-boned place in which they evolved, and my hope is that they will continue to headline Maximum Green Week and host old tractor-tire swings for another twelve thousand years (fig. 5).

Aesculus hippocastanum

horse chestnut

On Horse Chestnuts and Memory

Laurie Olin / Philadelphia, USA

58

Laurie Olin is a founding partner of OLIN
and a practice professor of landscape architecture
at the University of Pennsylvania.

1

1944. Discovery of nuts (seeds or conkers) on the ground while walking to and from first grade in Vancouver, Canada, age six: picking them up, feeling their smoothness, the glistening chestnut color—auburn, burnt sienna, with touches of maroon and Vandyke brown and a flattish base patch in matte dirty white—glistening shiny they filled my small hand, in a pocket. Surprised also by their shell (capsule), its open broken fleshy rubbery wrapper of the palest sickly milky lime green fading to pale lemon with sharp spikes spaced apart all over!

1961. The University of Washington in Seattle, where John Charles Olmsted (1852–1920) planted them after the Alaska-Yukon-Pacific Exposition along a campus drive that descends from Lewis and Clark Halls—after a long gray rainy winter, spring arrives. I am riding along, coasting on my bicycle beneath their canopy just under a sea of blossoms in the allée—sunlight in the spikes of upright creamy blossoms (erect panicles 10–30 cm tall) shedding petals (20–50 per plume) covering the street (fig. 1).

The fruit is Toxic to humans.

1967. Under Paris skies ("Sous le ceil de Paris" by Hubert Giraud and Jean Dréjac, recorded by Edith Piaf in 1954—hum a few bars), rainy autumn in the Tuileries, tobacco and gold, tan canopy above, a carpet of wet leaves on the gravel with a repetitive forest of black trunks extending into the distance à la Descartes's optics—implied infinity of the grid, a cathedral, simple palette: leaves above, leaves below, trunks in between, repeat—nuts and husks scattered about and once more picking several up, rubbing and inspecting them idly and finding them later in a pocket of a jacket on returning home (fig. 2).

1972. Revisit Paris, Tuileries, Jardin du Luxembourg—grand colonnades and bosques, quincunxes and allées of them, early autumn stately shedding and beautiful, the rows of wet dark straight trunks, ascending and descending branches, shuffling and scuffling leaves, gathering and pocketing a few more conkers (fig. 3).

Dan Kiley told me he measured the spacing of the horse chestnuts in the Tuileries and they were 14 feet 8 inches (447 cm) on center. Later I measured some there and in the Luxembourg Garden and found they varied from 427 to 487 cm or more.

1974. Discover on moving to Philadelphia a diagonal allée planted by Paul Philippe Cret (1876–1945) in Rittenhouse Square. Tall, straight, and graceful, with their lower branches drooping and then curling up at the end like monkey tails, smaller than those in Paris or England or Seattle—it's too hot, too southern in Philadelphia, not cool like Seattle, London, or Paris—still, there they are in spring with their beautiful blossoms and in fall with their sensual nuts.

Aesculus hippocastanum, no matter where it first evolved, in human—if not geological—time, is thought to have been native to a region extending from the Adriatic shore of the Balkans to the depths of Turkey. It can live to three hundred years.

2

2010. Working at the Château de Chantilly in Picardy, sorting out the traffic and parking, we manage to remove and relocate tourist bus and automobile parking from within the tall stately diagonal allées (on the roots) leading to André Le Nôtre's (1613–1700) entry to the château, restoring them to health and dignity (fig. 4).

I've planted their American cousins, Ohio buckeyes (*Aesculus glabra*), in

3

4

5

New York and Philadelphia, notably at Columbus Circle and the Barnes Foundation (fig. 5), along with European and Asian varieties.

Sadly, a lovely double row I planted in London has been cut down (along with complete demolition of my project) at Bishopsgate. They were thought messy. I'd hoped people coming down from their offices for fresh air and lunch in the autumn would see the conkers, stop, and idly pick one up, rub it, be flooded with some memory of their childhood, and stick it in their pocket before returning to their desks and computers.

However, many people, even professionals who should know better, dislike them and parrot the remark that they become desiccated and brown in mid- to late summer and look bedraggled. This is based upon the fact that many have been inappropriately planted in areas subject to high heat and decades of drought. When planted sensibly in cooler, moist climates in free-draining soils, they invariably thrive. There isn't a member of the horse chestnut family I don't think attractive (fig. 6). I love the red ones (*Aesculus ×carnea*), also from Europe, which are a bit smaller. One of the most beautiful sights I recall was of a mountain west of Beijing covered with a forest of Chinese chestnuts (*Castanea mollissima*)—but they are one of the edible species—in bloom in spring at the site of the monastery and grave of Kublai Khan's daughter.

1993. I discovered another thing I should have realized. There is an amusing variation in the number of leaflets (opposite, palmately compound) in their expansive, attractive sprays (figs. 7 and 8)—but then, why not? Nature loves to tease and please us with variations on a theme. One of my favorite variations on the organism TREE is definitely the noble horse chestnut.

6

7

Chestnut leaves from the Luxembourg. Funny, I'd always thought they were all the same, but of course there is variation, not only in the individual lobes, size and serration but in the very number of leaflets.

8

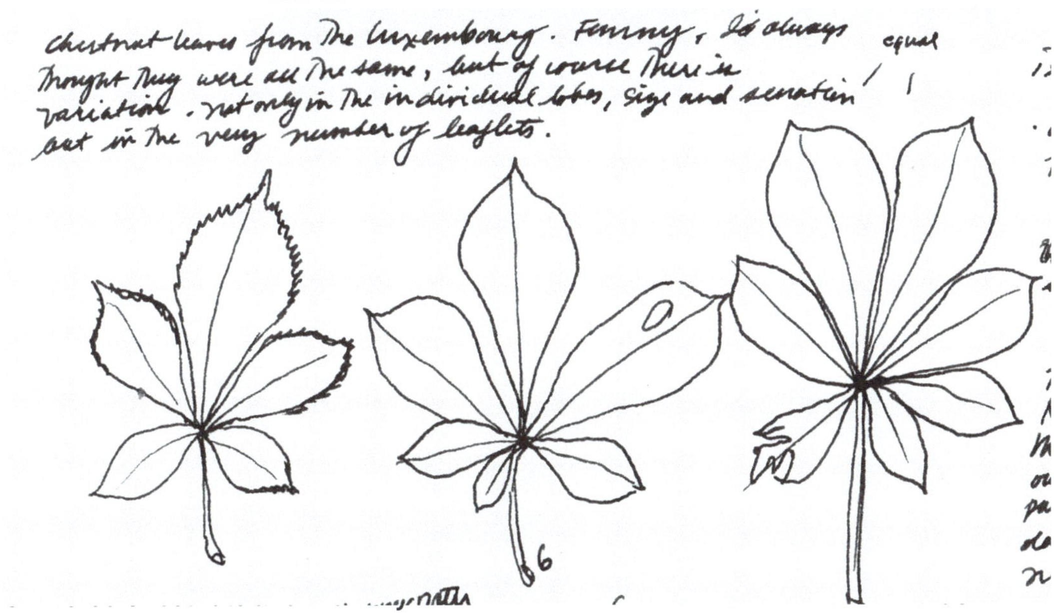

Betula pendula

European white birch

Figure, Light, and Illusion

Günther Vogt / Zurich, Switzerland

Günther Vogt is a professor of landscape architecture at ETH Zurich and founding principal of VOGT Landscape Architects.

Translated from the German by
Laura Schmidt and Johanna Bensch.

Christmas 1967. Many people have been struck by the spirit of the holidays: presents, peace, and family. Everything is ready for the party, except the Christmas tree. My mother asks my father to cut down a tree from our forest for the occasion. When we get to the forest, my father asks me which tree I want. I see a beautiful birch at the edge of the forest with bright white bark. That's my choice. Puzzled, he tells me a Christmas tree must be evergreen. I explain to him that the

1

2

white bark of the birch will make up for the lack of snow. We agree and head home with the tree. My mother's face falls when she sees it. But she manages to make it the most beautiful Christmas tree we've ever had.

Every tree species is unique. That means every project requires rediscovering what makes them special. Beech is a tree that doesn't have any prominent features, except when it gets old and develops a very individual and picturesque appearance. The leaves stay on the tree and change with the seasons. In spring, new leaves emerge and push out the old ones that have turned brown over time.

The Persian ironwood reveals an invisible weather phenomenon in its fall colors. Like a compass, these colors depend on sun exposure during the summer. Exposure: north, east, west, south. Leaves: yellow-green, yellow, orange, red.

Birches grow at the border between houses and meadows. On forgotten gravel, they propagate endlessly. In contrast, birches in private gardens are treated as specimen trees. They struggle to fulfill their natural habits due to competition from other species. The imaginary forest that lies behind the solitary tree is missing in these gardens.

Ecology. This branch of biology deals with biological, geological, and hydrological connections of organisms to one another. For example, why do we find birches on very wet land but also very dry land? Their ability to compete as a shade-intolerant tree species is not enough to dominate. They have been pushed out of high-quality sites by other trees. Birches are anemophilous and spread their seeds endlessly. Their life strategy is simple: grow fast and produce a lot of seeds. Almost every seed germinates. The saplings do not compete with one another for nutrients and space, and the tree provides

3

a habitat for many organisms: plants, fungi, and animals. And that includes butterflies.

Mimicry. The peppered moth's (*Biston betularia*) white wing color evolved to match birch bark, but when the environment changed due to the Industrial Revolution, climate change, and air pollutants, the peppered moth developed a darker color. On bark that was no longer white, it was better protected from predators. Birches can adapt quickly to dramatic environmental changes. In nuclear-polluted landscapes, like Chernobyl, such changes affect all native organisms. Evolution is usually a slow process, but at Chernobyl, new varieties of birches were found after only a few years.

Appearance. The white color of birch bark, produced by betulin, reflects sunlight during winter and summer to protect the trunks from sunburn. They need this protection because they are shade intolerant. The white bark peels off like pages of a book as the tree ages. Black horizontal stripes and lenticels contrast with the vertical texture of the slender trunk, created by light. In the open birch forest, oak and beech trees grow under the protection of the birches and eventually replace them as the final stage of the European forest. During the ice ages, birch, hazel, and alder were the primary species in the European landscape. The climate was similar to present-day Canada or Siberia. In these places, birches do not grow as solitary trees in gardens, but in dense groves or forests.

The foliage of the many trunks creates a delicate cover, with no shade. The shade in a birch forest depends on how far you go into it and how many trees there are. Like any forest, it offers protection and permanence. You can cut down the forest, but you cannot move it. It is a symbol that resembles an urban cityscape.

When you enter a dense forest, you see what is near, not what is far. You feel comfortable because you recognize trees from the city's parks and gardens and

meadows. But unlike any other forest, entering a birch forest is like stepping into another world: a sequence of rooms. The many trunks lose their individuality and together they form a room-like space. Inside and outside. Between these trunks, poetry emerges. The space between them creates the mystery of birch forests, something serene and not made by human hands.

4

5

Bursera simaruba

gumbo-limbo, copal, papelillo rojo, palo mulato

Giant Red Living Sculpture of the Mexican Deciduous Jungles

Mario Schjetnan / Mexico City, Mexico

72

Mario Schjetnan is a landscape architect, architect, and director of Grupo de Diseño Urbano (GDU) in Mexico City.

1 

2 

I first stumbled across a dense mass of beautiful, sculpted branches and trunks in deep rusty red with light green fronds from the majestic and monumental open-air "windows" in the lobby of the architect Ricardo Legorreta's Camino Real Hotel (now Las Brisas) in Ixtapa, Mexico, in the 1980s. They were tall, and planted close to the building, set against magnificent long views towards the western Sierra Madre mountains. I immediately asked what these beautiful trees were named; "papelillo rojo," I was told, or "palo mulato" (figs. 1 and 2). Since then, they have stuck in my mind as an iconic and distinctive image of the low deciduous jungles (LDJ) of Mexico.

Later, in the 1990s, I had the great opportunity to design a vast 80 ha site encompassing a nature reserve and archaeological ruins along the Copalita River in Bahías de Huatulco, on the Pacific coast of the Mexican state of Oaxaca. The master plan had been developed by the national tourism authority between 1981 and 1982 with significant landscape and environmental planning by Grupo de Diseño Urbano (GDU). The eco-archaeological reserve park, including a museum, was designed in 2008–10 by myself with the rest of the GDU. We worked together with biologists Alfredo Saynes and Emmanuelle Gamboa from the National Autonomous University of Mexico, experts on the LDJ biome, which occurs in the western Sierra Madre along the Pacific coastline from Sinaloa to Oaxaca. There, in addition to its incredible beauty, I learned more about the genus Bursera, which comprises around a hundred species endemic to the Americas, 80 percent of which thrive in Mexico.

The common name "copal" comes from the Nahuatl word *copalli* (incense); this resinous and aromatic wood has been used since pre-Hispanic times in religious ceremonies, celebrations, and purification offerings for health and well-being. It is still used today in churches and festival altars such as those for the Day of the Dead, a November festival of pre-Hispanic origin at which people celebrate and honor their deceased relatives.

More recently, GDU was the landscape architect for the new Four Seasons Tamarindo Hotel on the Pacific coast in the state of Jalisco, in collaboration with architects Víctor Legorreta and Mauricio Rocha and interior designer Uribe Krayer (fig. 3). The hotel sits on rugged terrain with magnificent elevated views of the ocean—with dramatic cliffs on one side and a long crescent beach bordering a small bay on the other. The rear looks toward a 15 km² private reserve of practically untouched hills of low deciduous jungle. When I first saw this magical site, it reminded me of the marvelous landscape descriptions in Herman Melville's novel *Typee*, set in the Marquesas Islands (fig. 4). An edition of the book from the 1930s is illustrated by one of my favorite twentieth-century artists/illustrators—the Mexican painter, caricaturist, illustrator, art historian, and anthropologist Miguel Covarrubias.

The design team defined the project as being about "absolute integration between the architecture and the jungle." Therefore, the impact from the clearings created for the buildings was to be offset by planting species endemic to the site: ozote (tree morning glory, *Ipomoea pauciflora*), guaje (white leadtree, *Leucaena leucocephala*), primavera (primrose, *Primula* sp.), coyul (*Pseudobombax* sp.), guayaco (lignum vitae, *Guaiacum officinale*), guamúchil (blackbead, *Pithecellobium* sp.), parota (*Enterolobium* sp.), coliguana (*Cordia* sp.), ceiba (kapok, *Ceiba pentandra*), and many others—and, of course the beautiful copal (*Bursera simaruba*), the dominant or codominant species of the LDJ biome.

Soon we learned, guided by the local biologist Francisco "Paco" Ramírez, that our favorite tree was easy to transplant from the site's nursery, and we carefully collected trees from the jungle reserve, repositioning each one with stakes. The beautiful, slim trunks were easy to move and plant in steep conditions as well as small patios or gardens (fig. 5). Copal grows fast and is easy to establish or adapt. It is resistant to hurricanes or tropical rainstorms. Surprisingly, it is a very difficult tree to find in commercial nurseries and therefore very rarely used in urban landscape projects, residential developments, and recreational projects along the Pacific coast.

We should plant more of them.

3

4

"vast roots of trees hung down from the sides of the ravine, dripping with moisture"

5

Ceiba pentandra

kapok, ceiba

Hope, Renewal, and Cosmography in the Americas

Roberto J. Rovira / Miami, USA, and Guayama, Puerto Rico

When I want to know myself, I read myself in the landscape.
That is what is important. Yes. The tree speaks to me.
I don't know if I can talk to the trees, but I know that they
speak to me and they interpret me

Aimé Césaire

Roberto J. Rovira is the chair of the Landscape Architecture + Environmental and Urban Design program at Florida International University and the principal of Studio Roberto Rovira in Miami.

The eruption of Mount Pelée on the Caribbean island of Martinique claimed over thirty thousand lives in 1902 but spared a kapok tree that would become a symbol of hope and solace for its prolific native son, Aimé Césaire, poet, statesman, humanist, and intellectual leader of the anticolonial Negritude movement, which in the 1930s sought to reclaim the value of Blackness and African culture (Bennett 2023).

Respect for the outsize majesty of the *Ceiba pentandra*, the largest tree of eighteen subspecies that natively grow in the Americas and West Africa, is broadly manifest in peoples across the neotropical regions of the world (Tareau et al. 2022). Also known as "silk-floss," the tree boasts mature heights of more than 50 m, often dramatically supported by a buttressed trunk that fans out from a thick central core (fig. 1). This exalted drought-tolerant species plays a prominent role in the origin stories and spiritual cosmography of many indigenous cultures from Central to South America and in my native Caribbean (fig. 2).

The primordial legacy of the kapok is connected to both creation and destruction, often acting as an inflection point for civilization and the ebb and flow of natural cataclysms, where an end begets an origin. For the Tikuna people of the Amazon basin, the cycle of primeval darkness was broken when a giant kapok was cut down to allow light to enter. The Peruvian Yagua and Ecuador's Huaorani attribute the Amazon itself to the felling of this giant tree, water from its trunk and branches spilling onto the land, the river's meandering arteries as proof. To the Wayana, a Carib-speaking people who live in the southeastern part of the Guiana highlands, the Milky Way is known as "the place where the ceiba was burned," its ashes visible as the stars where shamans

1

travel during trance. The Yawanawá village of Mutum in Acre, Brazil, calls its tree Samaúma (fig. 3).

The kapok also plays the role of national symbol, spiritual shelter, and grantor of wishes in Central America and the Caribbean. For the Miskito in Nicaragua and Honduras, the kapok is said to open a door to supplicants. Orisha spirits from the Yoruba religion of West Africa—and the Cuban, Dominican and Puerto Rican Santería religions that derived from it—are said to live in its trunk; fear of divine retribution protects the tree from being cut down.

2

As the national tree of my native Puerto Rico and a memorable setting for many unsupervised childhood adventures, my brothers and I played hide-and-seek around its massive trunk while avoiding the cows and horses who also sought shelter and shade from the tropical sun at my grandfather's farm. Growing up on the island's south coast, we made pilgrimages to the storied living landmark known as the Ceiba de Ponce (figs. 4A and 4B). This centuries-old specimen is thought to date back to before the 1700s and was celebrated by the Puerto Rican impressionist painter Francisco Oller in *La ceiba de*

Ponce in 1888. This kapok is in terminal decline despite attempts to support and revive its weakened limbs.

Kapoks are also identifiable by their stout conical thorns. Palmate leaves and flowers range from reds to pinks to

that—besides the practical use of kapok seeds for manufacturing soap, oil, and paint—about half a pound of kapok fruit fibers can keep a person afloat, which made those fibers a valuable raw material for life preservers.

yellows and whites depending on the species. The kapok often towers over adjacent canopies and thrives in seasonally dry tropical forests and subtropical regions.

During World War I, and up until my days as a Navy officer over three decades ago, the word "kapok" was synonymous with life preservers. It turns out

Material properties and versatility notwithstanding, the kapok's grandeur comes naturally with its colossal scale and millennial history, which grants it an outsize role in our collective memory and lived experience. As a symbol of resilience, hope, and renewal, it stands long after others have come and gone. Its history is a touchstone for the many

3

Ceiba pentandra

4A

cultures and individuals who have paid homage to this living giant through enduring stories transmitted from person to person and landscape to landscape over thousands of years.

4B

Bennett, S. 2023. "Aimé Césaire Kapok: The Tree That Inspired a Civil Rights Legend." Uncommon Caribbean. Last modified April 17, 2023. https://www.uncommoncaribbean.com/martinique/aime-cesaire-kapok/.

Tareau, M.-A., A. Greene, G. Odonne, and D. Davy. 2022. "*Ceiba pentandra* (Malvaceae) and associated species: Spiritual Keystone Species of the Neotropics." *Botany* 100, no. 2: 127–40.

Cercidiphyllum japonicum

katsura

Komorebi, an Ephemeral Pattern of Light and Shadow

Toru Mitani / Tokyo, Japan

Toru Mitani leads the Landscape Lab at the University of Tokyo's Department of Architecture and is founding partner of studio on site.

1

2

I came across katsura trees in my first project after returning to Japan from the United States. I had chosen a poplar tree for a project due to its strong verticality, but the garden contractor recommended katsura for its square shape, soft texture, and tolerance of the Japanese environment. I persisted in using poplars, and a typhoon in the first year destroyed them all. Katsura trees planted after that disaster easily avoided typhoons because of their flexible structure, and I have learned it is important to listen to contractors and gardeners.

The katsura taught me, a young landscape architect, by reminding me of lessons from professors. The tree's "form," or architecture, is fundamental for physical space-making, while characteristics like texture, seasonality, color, and biological

expression are more essential to create ephemeral qualities of landscapes. The katsura is always one of the best companions to realize both physical and phenomenal qualities.

Background and physical space-maker. Katsura are one of the most primitive trees surviving from the Cretaceous and Paleogene periods. Once widely distributed in the northern hemisphere, today they remain only in China and Japan. Two ancient documents, the *Kojiki* and the *Man'yōshū*, record that katsuras have been loved as a garden tree in Japan since the sixth century. They have straight trunks stretching toward the sky and dense horizontally spreading branches that give the tree an overall shape that is upright and ovate yet soft. Although in natural situations it is often multitrunked, it can grow into an upright single-trunk tree with proper management in urban projects. It is a prolific sprouter, with branches evenly distributed from the lower branches to the top and small, evenly distributed leaves.

Because of these architectural characteristics, I often use katsura to form rows or bosques (fig. 1). Rows of katsura effectively control large spaces as a green partition. Planted in groups as a bosque, it creates a strong sense of spatial perspective through the repetition of the trunks, while the fine, soft branches give the feeling of being enveloped in the clouds. Katsura are always effective for configuring both architectural and landscape-architectural space at the same time. With these physical characteristics, katsura is capable of creating a variety of impressive phenomena in the middle of cities.

A maker of ephemeral space. The fabric of *komorebi*, the pattern of light and shadow through leaves, is one of the charming phenomena of the katsura (figs. 2 and 3). Shinagawa Central Garden, designed and constructed from 1989 to 2002, is a bosque of 165 katsura, filling a space about 400 m long and 45 m wide (fig. 4). Wandering under these trees is like moving through a fine spray of light. This delicate fabric of light and shadow,

3

4

continually produced by the fluttering of the leaves in response to the slightest breeze, creates a space that can be described as an accumulation of minute fluctuations.

Although the bosque has such a delicate texture, in autumn it asserts a bold mass of orange and yellow color. Autumn may be the best season to witness a special katsura show. On the other hand, some may object that the best season is early summer, when the katsura's young leaves emerge bright green under the blue sky as if the gods are pulling them from a box of crayons. I propose, however, that late winter is the best season for katsura's charm. During a few weeks right before budding, a fog of coppery-red color

drifts in front of the buildings: a cloud of the small, dense buds and twigs of the katsura (figs. 5, 6, and 7).

A maker of cultural space. Katsura have been loved in Japan since ancient times, and the tree is considered auspicious. In Chinese folklore, it is believed that there is a giant katsura on the moon, and it has also been associated with celestial bodies and outer space in Japan. The famous Katsura Imperial Villa in Kyoto is so named because the concept of the garden is to transfer the moon to the pond for viewing.

Katsura leaves have the shape of a heart, which is said to be a symbol of the spirit of matchmaking. The space I designed for the approach to the garden of the Shimane Museum of Ancient Izumo is laid out in three rows of seventeen katsura to establish a sense of depth connecting to the mountain range behind the museum. It was surprising, after the construction was completed, to see a number of couples using this space to take commemorative photos of their marriage. This is a testament to the cosmic spirit that Japanese people still expect from the katsura.

Katsura do not have spectacular flowers or striking figures, but they possess all the other characteristics of a landscape space-maker. Visiting Shinagawa Central Garden on a summer evening, you will recognize, even in the city, that you are surrounded by the singing of crickets spread out across the bosque. Katsura are trees of subtle character that stand steadfastly by your side to reflect the breadth of the universe.

5
6
7

Cupressus sempervirens

Mediterranean cypress

Icon of the Mediterranean Landscape

Jordi Barri / Barcelona, Spain

Jordi Barri is an agricultural and forest engineer, landscape architect, and architect. He is the founder of Barri Studio in Barcelona.

As a child, wandering amidst the cypress seedlings in my father's nursery (fig. 1), I recall the invigorating scent—a blend of freshness, balsam, and subtle sweetness—lingering in the air. I can still feel the resinous texture of their leaves, as they imprinted themselves upon my hands when gently caressed.

Come March, a fine yellowish film of pollen would coat everything. With the summer sun, I would watch the cones swell, mature, and gradually darken to a rich brown, signaling the time for harvest. In our nursery, mature trees stood as natural protective barriers, their rows a shield for the glazed greenhouses (fig. 2). Thanks to the dense and elastic composition of the cypress, its pliant branches can bend without snapping, displaying remarkable resilience.

My task was to gather cones from a tree stationed at the entrance of our nursery house—a cherished tradition in Catalonia, where homes welcome visitors with cypresses symbolizing hospitality, a custom believed to date back to Roman times.

Botanically, the cypress is a monoecious plant, boasting both male and female cones on the same individual. Wind-borne pollen from the male cones settles upon the female cones, facilitating

1

2

the fertilization of seeds. Thus, a solitary cypress can produce new seeds without external pollination. The female cones often perched atop the trees, compelling me to venture onto the second-floor terrace of our house to collect them without mishap. Some cones, though intended for other purposes, turned into perfect projectiles for our children's games. The already-ruptured brown cones were placed in trays of water to be soaked for a day when immediate sowing was

3

4

5

6

7

7

necessary, although their seeds could endure for over a year. At home, we would sow them in enclosed beds crafted from ceramic masonry, filled with porous soil and sand, ensuring efficient drainage. The nursery brimmed with these beds, teeming with cypresses of various sizes—readied for transplantation or sale—and providing me with endless avenues for play and exploration.

This early encounter with *Cupressus sempervirens* shattered my preconceived notions of what a tree should be. With no sprawling canopy, no seasonal foliage metamorphosis, and no ostentatious blossoms, the cypress possessed a distinctive architectural allure (fig. 3). Yet, precisely due to its idiosyncratic form, this emblematic tree has captivated Mediterranean culture for centuries, gracing literature, poetry, painting, mythology, and religion (fig. 4).

A cultural symbol of the collective imaginary. As I journeyed through my formative years, I gradually grasped the deeper cultural significance associated with the presence of cypresses in distinctive locations such as cemeteries. These tall and slender trees held a profound meaning in ancient Greece and Rome, where they were purposefully planted as an emblem of everlasting life. Their lofty stature and slender form served as a poignant reminder of the ethereal connection bridging the earthly realm and the celestial sphere. We could add that the deep anchoring of the roots prevents any potential damage to the graves. Nevertheless, their influence extended far beyond the limits of the tangible, as in the inspirational pictorial world of the Catalan modernist painter and poet Santiago Rusiñol (1861–1931). He was renowned for his use of color and light in his famous series of landscape paintings of Mallorca and his drawings of cypress trees (fig. 5).

The versatility of cypress in landscape architecture. Today, as a landscape designer, I find the cypress's wide range of applications in landscape fascinating, from the foliage density and conical shape that make it an excellent visual and acoustic screen to the malleability that allows it to be molded into various shapes, turning it into an attractive sculptural element. It also stands out for emphasizing focal points and adding height to the landscape, highlighting verticality in the design.

If you travel to Tuscany, you will see how they create beautiful cultural landscapes through the rhythm of their plantings, such as lines of trees that mark the way to towns or villages (fig. 6). In addition, cypresses create spaces by visually relating to each other (fig. 7). One example is how the landscape architect Fernando Caruncho, known for his minimalist style and the focus on geometry and architecture in his designs, uses cypress trees to create a sense of order and architectural balance (fig. 8).

However, the current naturalistic trend in landscaping represents a move away from rigid geometry, giving priority to the creation of a natural environment that embraces an uncluttered elegance and a harmonious interplay of species in this ecosystem. This is how we prefer to plant them today, in a dispersed manner, paying tribute to this hardy, vigorous, evergreen, elegant, undervalued, and often forgotten tree, which serves as a common thread from the plantings of my earliest childhood to the present day as a landscape designer with the responsibility of bringing meaning and beauty to our ever-evolving landscapes.

8

Cyrtophyllum fragrans

tembusu, ironwood

Of Trees, Life, and Politics

Leonard Ng / Singapore

96

Leonard Ng is the country market director for the Asia-Pacific region at Henning Larsen and a practicing landscape architect based in Singapore.

The tembusu is close to my heart. The one featured on our Singaporean five-dollar banknote is the same one that I used to climb as a child, sitting on the horizontal branch with my siblings, our feet dangling in the air. It is also the first tembusu to be granted "heritage tree" status by the National Parks Board (fig. 1).

Trees have played a significant role in Singapore's development into a leading global nation in one generation. This is reflected in the evolution of Singapore's vision for itself, from "Garden City" to "City in a Garden" to the current "City in Nature." Given the multitude of tree species, both local and imported, planted amidst dense urbanity, it is notable that the tembusu was voted the city's "unofficial national tree" in an informal poll conducted in 2002 by Singapore's Nature Society.

The decade spanning 1965 to 1975 was a tumultuous and uncertain period in the newly independent Singapore, with my peers the first postcolonial generation after British rule. We were finding our way as a nation, with few resources except a young population. Our then prime minister, Lee Kuan Yew, had initiated the Garden City concept to attract multinational companies to invest and create jobs in Singapore.

The tembusu was identified as a suitable species during the early years of our greening movement due to its large mature size and excellent quality of shade. The tembusu's dainty creamy white flowers have been described as smelling "somewhat like jasmine, but without any indolic tendencies. There is a little sweet lemon freshness mixed with the floral jasmine smell. Some people say they can smell a touch of vanilla. ... It is like the freshest, sweetest jasmine you've ever smelt and its scent is euphoric."

1

It has such local significance that it was "used as a metaphor for relations between the state and civil society in the 1990s. In a 1998 speech, ambassador-at-large Tommy Koh likened the government under the premiership of Goh Chok Tong to the tembusu for its tall and strong qualities but with a canopy smaller than the banyan tree, which described the preceding Lee Kuan Yew era. The smaller canopy of the tembusu allows other plants—a reference to civil society—to grow around it" (Koh B. S. 1998).

The tembusu is a slow-growing evergreen tree native to many regions in tropical Asia, including Singapore. With time, it can reach a height of 40 m. Among its unique physical attributes are its dark brown and deeply fissured bark and high-quality timber suitable for construction (fig. 2).

E. J. H. Corner, in his seminal work *Wayside Trees of Malaya* (1952, 468), described the tembusu in almost human-like terms: "The tembusu responds very slowly to the climatic stimulus, its flowers opening after an interval of nearly four months. But in all its activities the tree is leisurely. It grows slowly; it develops new leaves a pair at a time, never in flush like so many of our eager trees: its flower-buds need several weeks to open; its flowers last for several days and are not morning-glories or night-dreams like so many others; and the tiny berries require more than three months to mature. Such sluggishness is remarkable in a tropical plant, the environment of which imposes no hindrance upon its growth, but it is not unparalleled for both Mangosteen and Nutmeg are almost, if not quite, as lethargic" (fig. 3).

Ironically, a tembusu was also responsible for generating much discussion about the maintenance of trees in urban areas. During an outdoor concert at the Singapore Botanic Gardens in 2017, a tembusu collapsed onto a crowded lawn, pinning a mother of two, which resulted in her death. That tree was then estimated to be more than 270 years old and held heritage tree status. Writing for Yahoo News, journalist Wan Ting Koh (2018) reported on allegations that the responsible government agency had not properly maintained the tree, thus subjecting the public to danger. Subsequently the court passed a verdict of "tragic misadventure," thereby absolving the agency of any liability for the woman's death. After consideration of expert testimony, it was determined that the event could not have been reasonably predicted.

As we realize the value of providing spaces for nature within our expanding cities, how do we deal with these unfortunate and unpredictable events? The knee-jerk response is to cull or remove any offending nonhuman nature, be it a tree or a fox. This incident involving the tembusu encapsulates the dilemma of both our love and fear for nature. How we resolve this quandary will have a far-reaching impact for the future of all living things (fig. 4).

Corner, E. J. H. 1952. *Wayside Trees of Malaya*. Singapore: Government Printing Office.

Cynthia. 2016. "Tembusu, Singapore's Fragrant Tree." *The Fragrant Journey*. May 18, 2016. https://thefragrantjourney.blogspot.com/2016/05/tembusu-singapores-fragrant-tree.html.

Koh B. S. 1998. "More Space in Tembusu Era." *Straits Times*, May 8, 1998, 55.

Koh, W. T. 2018. "Tembusu Tree Fall: Death of Woman Ruled a Tragic Misadventure." Yahoo News, April 30, 2018. https://sg.news.yahoo.com/tembusu-tree-fall-death-woman-ruled-tragic-misadventure-084252507.html.

2

3

4

Ficus carica

common fig

The One-Tree Courtyard

Andrew Todd / Blanot and Paris, France

100

Andrew Todd is an architect whose professional practice, Studio Andrew Todd, is deeply experienced in wood construction and in making theaters and performance spaces for the social arts.

A small courtyard was formed by the extensive overhaul (and healing) of a rural, war-traumatized Burgundy ballroom and residence, where I now dwell. Acting as the extension of a new kitchen and dining room, flanking a former barn-become-hovel, and bracketed on the other sides by stone retaining walls, the courtyard, at 450 × 475 cm, was too confined to be a proper outdoor room on its own merits. A further *dramatis persona* was called for: to stand up, to stand in, to hold court (so to speak) (fig. 1).

1

She is a fig tree who grew up among battalions of commercial saplings in the lush Arno valley between Florence and Pisa and moved to the Aosta valley to harden at a higher altitude. Word was sent through the grapevine of our local tree nursery that someone rather optimistic (me) was looking for a 5 m-high specimen with the lowest branches at 2.5 m and a crown diameter of 4 m maximum. We had almost given up looking—and were prepared to plump for a Japanese maple instead—but the adoption papers came through, and she arrived at the winter solstice (as it happened, a year to the day before my father died) in a huge 280 L pot, her branches wrapped in pigtails.

A hole was dug the night before, on an axis with the kitchen and the enlarged window of the (drastically improved) hovel perpendicular to it. We hoisted her over the neighbors' wall with a digger I had flagged down in the street, based on a promise of wine and cash. I sat in the clawed mouth of the bucket and undid her hair-ties from above. She went "ptoing" and shook her barnet. It was snowing and the hole prepared for her was filling in; there were only a couple of minutes to decide which aspect best suited her stage set—a fraught choice, as her pigtails were still slowly unfolding into their resting, long-haired shape. The digger driver had to scoot, so she settled rather by default, raised slightly above grade by the snow and mud that had accumulated, forming a kind of tumulus around her trunk that was accidental and—it soon transpired—portentous.

We named her Florence and, it turns out, she brought some baggage. As her leaves swelled into large, rough, triple-lobed solar panels, it became plausible that Adam and Eve had sewn them together to fashion the first clothes as they became aware of their nakedness. The impossibly raunchy fruit was compared lasciviously to female genitals by Alan Bates's Rupert Birkin in Ken Russell's film *Women in Love*. Small wonder, then, that some biblical scholars have deemed the tree of the knowledge of good and evil to be of the ficus family.

Judas hanged himself from a fig tree, something rather hard to believe as their branches are extremely elastic, bowing down in midsummer under the weight of fat fruits. More auspiciously, the Buddha attained enlightenment at the foot of a banyan (Bengal fig), and Krishna was born inside one, where his mother was sheltering from the tyrant Kansa. In ancient Egypt, the goddess Hathor had a fig tree whose branches were full of the bodies of the dead, which took the form of birds. Having been admitted to paradise, the fig fruit was their reward. The goddess Sefkhet wrote the deeds and stories of the life of each dead human on fig leaves, one leaf per life.

I was pleased that the new arrival was overweeningly pregnant with mythological agency; my personal favorite story is from Georgia: unborn babies are held by its branches, which bend to lower them into a surrounding lake of milk, lifting them out to be plucked by their parents when ripe. As I soon discovered when picking an underripe fruit, the fig produces a caustic white latex sap, used traditionally in Chad to stimulate lactation by rubbing it on women's nipples.

Her new home was a success, maybe too much so. Florence shot out roots and got shaggy up top. In the first year she produced a large but rather insipid first harvest. In year three there was a terrible frost in late April that devastated the crops of our nearby winemaker friends. Florence had her buds out, and my wife kept vigil in the courtyard with a night barbecue to raise the temperature above freezing. It worked for the bottom half of the branches, leaving Florence with the look of a tonsured monk as the leaves emerged. Returning from holiday a month later, the top half suddenly decided to spurt upwards, and she looked for all the world like the lumpy bouffant of Nigel Tufnel in the movie *This Is Spinal Tap*.

When she gives forth, it's all at once, plethoric. Gorging on fresh fruit for days, we run out of steam after the second batch of chutney and jam. There being five fig trees in the village, hardly anyone else wants the bounty either. Then, every February, I have the fraught task of pruning, an exercise in four-dimensional divination, after the last hard frost, final form unfolding according to climate and the energy levels of the tree in springtime. The pruning produces a set of antlers, as if there had been a tree-rut. Left to her own devices, she would swell and take over the house. Our shared life is a (slow) conversation, a negotiation, a dance, an origin renewed every year.

And, since joining the family, Florence has instructed us in some of the weightier aspects of life. My father visited (on his last trip) in May of the year after adoption. At that time the microfigs (actually introverted flowers) adorned the dry branches like tiny caper berries, the baby leaves—no bigger than a fingertip—striving for the sun. When he died six months later a part of his ashes came here for burial at the foot of the tree, in the tumulus. The axis established by Florence in the dining room made for a perfect ritual space, the precious dust in a bowl flanked by candles on the table, his image open in a book before it (fig. 2).

We repeated the same ceremony two years later for our beloved dog Suki. Another two years and we would find ourselves there in intense reflection, savoring a Château Latour 2016 Beaune Perrières Premier Cru in memory of another habitué of the courtyard, the winemaker's brother, philosopher Bruno Latour.

Woody plants and their contexts were—in many ways—the foundation of Latour's thought. Having grown up with his hands in the Burgundy soil, he was primed to step sideways from the Parisian establishment that had ignored him for so many years; he was also personally attuned to more-than-human life cycles, the question of landing here and now on a contested earth becoming the center of his late work. He was worried about Suki (she died ten days after his visit). Concerning Florence, he carefully contemplated her from various angles, and then adjudged: “She’s well placed.”

2

Ficus macrophylla

Moreton Bay fig

Forest Giants in the City

Elizabeth Mossop / Sydney, Australia

104

Elizabeth Mossop is a professor of landscape architecture, the dean of the Faculty of Design, Architecture and Building at the University of Technology Sydney, and a founding principal of Spackman Mossop Michaels Landscape Architects.

1

It seems counterintuitive that the Moreton Bay fig, native to Australia's east coast rainforest, and named for a place 1,000 km away, reminds me of my home city, Sydney. The tree has two forms, neither of which seem ideally suited to city life at first glance. In the rainforest it is a strangler fig: the seed germinates in the canopy of a host, growing epiphytically while sending roots to the ground, eventually enveloping (and killing) the host and becoming freestanding. When planted, however, it is one of the most magnificent and gigantic specimen trees. In Sydney it has become a characteristic element of urban parklands, especially in the city and the historic harborside parks of the downtown. There is nothing like these trees: their scale, glossy leaves, and curvaceous sculptural trunks. When mixed with other trees it is the figs that give Sydney its subtropical and slightly exotic feeling.

You can walk around inside them and be enveloped by the canopy. They can grow 60 m high and 35 m in height and spread—and can spread across a hectare. Everything about them is large. The name is from the Ancient Greek *macros* (large) and *phyllon* (leaf). The leaves are ovals up to 250 mm in length, thick and shiny green on top and rusty underneath (fig. 1).

Figs are unique, as their flower is enclosed in the fruit. Open a fig up and see hundreds of florets inside. Figs have a symbiotic relationship with the tiny native Moreton Bay fig wasp (*Pleistodontes froggatti*). The wasp enters a hole at the end of the fruit and lays eggs inside to pollinate the flower. The hole seals up and the fruit develops. The fruits are edible, but not delicious for human consumption, being rather dry and made up of gritty seeds. They provide plentiful food for native birds and animals such as pigeons, parrots, flying foxes, and possums.

2

While the canopy and figs are beautiful, it is the form of the skeleton that most distinguishes these trees. Their armature is huge and muscular; trunks commonly grow up to 2.5 m in diameter. They are adapted to grow in nutrient-poor soils—often beginning their lives germinating in rocky crevices or the canopy of another tree—and have developed aerial roots to take up nutrients and moisture from the air. These roots grow down from the branches and into the ground, forming "buttress" roots that then support the tree in continuous serpentines curving across the ground that merge into the trunk and into the sky along the branches (fig. 2).

There are magnificent specimens in all of the east coast botanic gardens and across Sydney's major historic parks. I often walk in Jubilee Park, where one of my favorites can be found at the end of Glebe Point, extending from the waterfront to the road with its arms spread out as a capacious outdoor living room (fig. 3).

Before the Sydney Olympics, we designed a new urban park between the Catholic cathedral and the natural history museum downtown. Cook and Phillip Park was created on a sloping site from a series of underused streets and a lawn bowls club. One of the streets had a significant avenue of mature Moreton Bay figs, and this beautiful curved avenue is preserved in the new design, providing a dramatic diagonal slicing through the park's lawn terraces (fig. 4).

These trees were planted originally as street trees, probably in the 1860s under the influence of Charles Moore, director of the nearby Royal Botanic Garden from 1848 to 1896. As the park was developed in the late 1990s, the figs were carefully protected from demolition, and new works used pinpoint supports to bridge across the root systems without damage. The trees have responded well to the removal of the pavement around them and flourished in the park environment.

Our city regulators and municipal landscape "police" regard them as too

3

large for our cities and suburbs. Where we used to plant wonderful street trees, we now plant overgrown shrubs that do little to help our urban environments. While it is true these fig trees are huge and have spreading root systems, it is not difficult to account for this in designing roads and public landscapes. We have all the appropriate urban technology and know-how to accommodate tree canopies and their root systems as well as municipal services.

These are some of the very few trees of a scale to hold their own against urban infrastructure and help reduce its unfriendly dominance of urban spaces. We need to restore nature in our cities in a powerful way so that trees like this can have as strong a presence as buildings.
4 We can't just use plants as the polite decoration of our built structures (fig. 5).

As many cities, like Sydney, become hotter, climate adaptation requires we plant many shade trees. Spreading canopies with dense shade are required to lower urban temperatures. Most of our indigenous trees, like eucalypts, provide little density of shade or spread of coverage. Our existing historical plantings of figs demonstrate just how well-suited they are to provide this shade and how much they can lower temperatures.

It's time we prioritize shade, biodiversity, contact with nature, and beauty. We need to return to planting significant trees like the Moreton Bay fig and welcome them again to the heart of our cities.

5

Gleditsia triacanthos

honey locust

The Finely Textured Canopy of Modernism

Ron Henderson / Chicago, USA

Ron Henderson is a professor in the Landscape Architecture + Urbanism program at the Illinois Institute of Technology and founding principal of LIRIO Landscape Architecture.

1

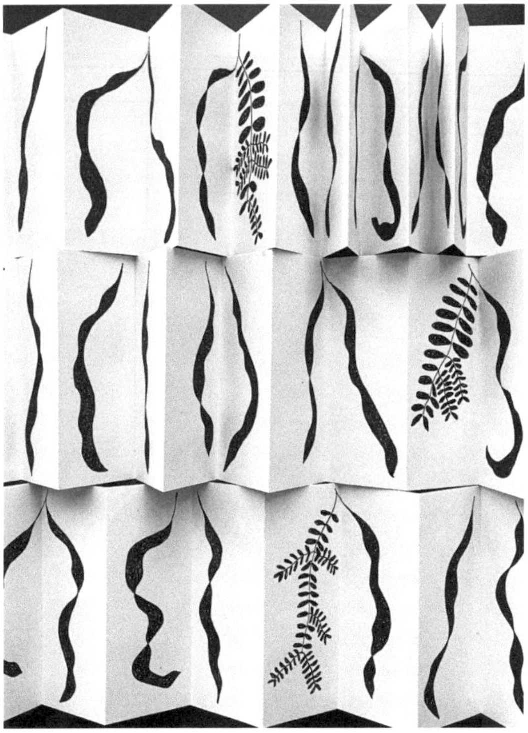

Giant sloths and mastodons feasted on the sweet pods of the honey locust. With the demise of these megafauna, the honey locust's native range shrank, as the seeds became less viable and less mobile. Today, the native range of the honey locust is centered in the limestone valleys and sinkholes along the Ohio River in the American Midwest. It was here, in the Midwest in the 1950s and 1960s, that the honey locust started its ascendance as a tree with desirable design characteristics: picturesque branching habit, diaphanous open canopy, vibrant yellow fall foliage, course platelets of textured bark, and small oblong-lanceolate leaflets that scatter in the wind, which I frequently draw in orihon folding sketchbooks (fig. 1).

"There is a certain refinement about this tree, and in its golden-yellow autumn color it gives a soft light to the landscape," wrote landscape architect Jens Jensen in his 1939 book *Siftings* (48). Jensen had notably planted a group of four honey locusts at each of the path intersections in the vegetable garden at the Edsel and Eleanor Ford House outside Detroit in 1927. The honey locust's open canopy of pinnate and bipinnate leaves provided some shade but did not obstruct light from the ground, so that other plants could grow beneath it. Alfred Caldwell worked for Jensen on this project and would become one of two landscape architects—Dan Kiley being the other—most associated with this species over the subsequent modernist decades.

Caldwell was the first American faculty member hired by Ludwig Mies van der Rohe at the Illinois Institute of Technology,

2

3

and the two would collaborate on its campus for almost two decades. Their first collaboration, in 1954, included a collection of American elms, honey locusts, and crabapples loosely enclosing a "play meadow" at the university's new high-rise through the diaphanous canopy into the column-free room: the finely textured canopy of modernism.

A few years earlier, in 1949, a thornless, seedless variety of the species was patented by the Siebenthaler Nursery

4

housing. The American elm was being decimated by Dutch elm disease, and these would be the last elms planted on the campus for over half a century.

When Caldwell completed the planting around IIT's Crown Hall a few years later, the species list only included honey locusts and crabapples. Caldwell purposely selected gnarly specimens so their form would contrast with the cubic orthogonality of Mies's steel-and-glass building. Caldwell's selection of the honey locust reverberates powerfully—in twisted shadows projected on translucent glass (fig. 2), in sharp fluorescent green and emergent crimson thorns pointing toward charcoal-steel columns (fig. 3), in colorful golden-yellow reflections cast upon polished terrazzo, and in sunlight passing

Company in Dayton, Ohio. *Gleditsia triacanthos* var. *inermis* "Moraine" became the first patented shade tree in North America when it was issued US Plant Patent 836 almost two decades after the Plant Patent Act of 1930. It was the new variety of honey locust that landscape architect Dan Kiley selected for the Miller Garden in Columbus, Indiana (fig. 4). In contrast with Caldwell's irregularly spaced groves and thorny specimens, Kiley arrayed the tree in an orderly allée. This iconic planting of honey locusts is positioned parallel with the west facade of the house to establish an arboreal loggia overlooking the expansive lawn, which recedes down to a wooded riverbank. The trees of this allée have been replaced twice over the past seventy years. In each case, all of the trees were removed and new, matching specimens planted.

In contrast, the irregularly spaced (and thorny) honey locusts of IIT (and other Caldwell projects at Lafayette Park in Detroit and Skyline Park in Chicago) largely persist. However, over the last two decades, landscape architects Peter Lindsay Schaudt, Chandra Goldsmith Gray, and I have each worked to diversify the tree collection on the IIT campus (fig. 5). Today, the campus is an arboretum with a particularly strong collection of pinnate leaf species with yellow fall foliage: Kentucky coffee tree, black walnut, shagbark hickory, yellowwood, black locust, and a few green and white ash that are surviving the emerald ash borer infestation. At Crown Hall, it is the Kentucky coffee tree (*Gymnocladus dioicus*) that most closely replicates the characteristics of the honey locust.

Today, the durable honey locust comprises almost a third of all street trees in Chicago, as it does in many other American cities. Yet it is good to see beyond their current ubiquity and remember their inestimable design characteristics. How wonderful, Caldwell mused in a 1996 conversation with his IIT colleague Kevin Harrington, to see the world that filters through their canopy of leaves, "a kind of mysterious continuum of light and shadow."

5

Jensen, J. 1939. *Siftings*. Chicago: Ralph Fletcher Seymour.

Handroanthus serratifolius

curarire, ipê, poui, pau d'arco

Colloquy beneath the One with Yellow Flowers

Maria A. Villalobos H. / Puerto de Altagracia, Venezuela

116

To my mother, Zoila Antonia Hernandez Romero de Villalobos

Maria A. Villalobos H. is an associate professor at the Illinois Institute of Technology. She holds a master's in design studies from the Harvard Graduate School of Design and a PhD in landscape architecture from the ENSP in Versailles. She is the founder of Botanical City and a core member of Dark Matter University.

I recall listening to Andrés Eloy Blanco on my home's patio. The colloquies beneath the laurels, palms, cypresses, and acacias awakened my curiosity because they eloquently portrayed the interplay between time's abundance and life's urgent nature. My mother continues to recite those poems, and their resonance echoes through the corridors of time. As I matured, a tapestry of symbols unfolded. "La matica" by Un Sólo Pueblo became recurrent. The song—whose name means "the little plant"—stirred my father's soul in unspoken depths, concealing reasons within. This botanical anthem celebrates a plant, a stubborn dwelling, defying drought, forever verdant, imbued with divine fortitude and boundless generosity. Thus, from the silence of childhood, my brother and I gained insight, recognizing the value of flexibility, strength, and growth, even amidst the harshest drought. This revelation confirmed that the brilliance of freedom remains indomitable, impervious to any attempt by authority to quell it.

Growing up by the lake, we became travelers by joyful fate. Just like our Guajiro ancestors, we too embodied the essence of nomadism, where travel becomes an avenue for experiencing, decision-making, and embracing life itself (fig. 1). My brother painted landscapes

1

2

inside *totumas* (gourd bowls), crafted stained glass, and played the saxophone with the town band all around the lake. To study architecture, I crossed Lake Maracaibo by boat or car on routes that took two hours in each direction. There, for six months, the landscape lies dormant until March unfolds. Then, like a mesmerizing spectacle, the golden lights of blooming curarires (*Handroanthus serratifolius*), close relatives of the esteemed national tree of Venezuela, the araguaney (*Handroanthus chrysanthus*), illuminate the horizon, especially during our family excursions to Consejo de Ciruma to visit the Church of Saint Anthony. Years later, I came across Rómulo Gallegos calling it "The Golden Spring," adding a new global layer of meaning, and understood that little tropical girls like me in Africa, Asia, and Oceania were experiencing the same. Thus, the lake's travelers witnessed hope through the trees yearly, transcending intricate biological concepts and evoking an irresistible emotion. I dedicated my first academic thesis to the routes connecting Altagracia and Maracaibo through landscape formations where the curarires played the leading role. I envisioned the love that would stir within all travelers as they witnessed each blooming (fig. 2). As my thesis ranked among the nation's top ten, I exhibited it on the walls of Caracas's Museum of Fine Arts at age eighteen, accompanied by my mother. At that moment I grasped the power of the message, originating from a place where solitude appeared immutable and ageless. It became evident that awakening curiosity required not only the ice of the Gypsies but, above all, the resolute will to cultivate the legacy of our ancestors: curarires, cujíes (*Prosopis juliflora*), and ceibas (*Ceiba pentandra*).

Decades later, I heard Professor Daniel H. Janzen from the University of Pennsylvania reveal that my dry forest was the most threatened tropical ecosystem in the world and possessed the greatest capacity for climate adaptation. It brings a lump to your throat when science confirms the knowledge passed down to you

3

by your parents, people, and lake, far from numbers and maps and near poetry and travels. This awareness played a pivotal role in my contribution to preserving the tropical dry forest celebrated by Roberto Burle Marx, Leandro Aristeguieta, and their collaborators on Maracaibo's Botanic Garden (fig. 3). I gleaned firsthand that the curarires and their fellow beings carry three crucial messages. Firstly, I understood the connection between ancestral respect and the gradual demise of totalitarianism as commitments unfold across vast spans of space and time. Secondly, I experienced how freedom resides within the creative process, which defies the idea of a mere "project" or linear advancement and beckons collective enthusiasm free from the burdens of guilt or pettiness. Finally, I witnessed preservation through transformation, where individuals undergo personal growth while directing methodologies toward transmitting knowledge rather than seeking to control it (fig. 4).

Today, past the accolades adorning the walls for work done well, a wave of emotion floods my being when the garden and towns around the lake bloom. I remember the child who felt like ropes bursting with joy at every "Golden Spring," willing to do anything to safeguard her father's *matica*, knowing that it would forever inspire the colloquies of her mother. The invention of new colloquies for new children continues here with this imaginary collaboration with the master Andrés Eloy Blanco, a risk I lovingly take upon myself, based on his poem "Coloquio bajo la acacia" (Colloquy beneath the acacia):

And when all the trees of the earth are loved,
One tree is loved, a single tree, the fullness of a tree,
One tree is loved in two or a thousand or one,
And it is said, "My trees" or "My tree,"
Tree, in the function of all the loneliness in the world,
Tree at once and the truth of the tree;
My tree in twos, my solitary tree
Like the multitude of trees,
The trees of today in a garden
And along the paths of a long journey.

4

Liquidambar styraciflua

sweetgum

Crescendo of Color

Cannon Ivers / London, UK

120

Cannon Ivers is a director at LDA Design in London and a teaching fellow at the Bartlett School of Landscape Architecture.

The American sweetgum and I have something in common. We both immigrated to England, put down roots, and established ourselves in a new climate and cultural landscape. *Liquidambar* translates as "liquid amber," referencing the sweet resin that courses through the tree. Linnaeus named the genus from the Latin *liquidus* (fluid) and the Arabic *ambar* (amber). In 1519 a Spanish conquistador noted in his diary that he had observed Native Americans using sweetgum resin in ceremonies and for dental hygiene. The sweetgum was introduced to England from Virginia in 1683 by the plant collector John Banister (1654–92) and planted in Fulham Palace in London by Bishop Henry Compton (1632–1713). Banister was accidentally shot and killed on a plant-hunting expedition by a fellow plant hunter at age forty-two, and the sweetgum at Fulham Palace has also been lost, albeit under less tragic circumstances. Since its introduction to England, this upright and handsome species has been dazzling streets, parks, and squares with its unrivaled autumn display. Seemingly capable of showcasing every color simultaneously, it is a species that stops people in their tracks and reminds us every year to cherish the seasons and the passing of time.

Landscape architects Reed Hilderbrand positioned seven *Liquidambar* trees within the courtyard of the Naito and Bauer laboratories at Harvard University. The space has a strong diagonal path that responds to the pedestrian desire line and allows people to easily move from place to place. I can remember when the sweetgums were undergoing their annual kaleidoscopic transformation, and how my pace would slow as I made my way to the Graduate School of Design, observing others stopping, commenting, photographing, and sharing images on social media. The show-stopping display of color prompted people to comment on the beauty before them, building a moment of community cohesion that might have otherwise been absent as people hurried through the space. It was a great example of what William H. Whyte referred to as "triangulation," the character of a space that brings people together (fig. 1).

For me as a practicing landscape architect based in London, the sweetgum

1

2

is a go-to species that has featured in many of my projects. At Strand Aldwych I planted a line of 9 m-tall *Liquidambars* to give definition to the space, obscure the bright red London buses, and set benches beneath the colorful canopies (fig. 2). The crescendo of color adds something special as a distinct departure from the adjacent London planetrees. At Beresford Square in Woolwich, two specimen sweetgums have been carefully positioned to frame the adjacent, historically important Gatehouse, which was the formal entry to the Royal Arsenal at Woolwich (fig. 3). The tree canopies sit above an intimate garden that will work in tandem with the sweetgums as the planting and trees change collectively with the seasons. At Burgess Park in London we created two signature entrances with bespoke gates and hydric gardens. Sweetgums were selected for their ability to have their feet wet in the garden after a cloudburst and be equally happy in drier conditions. The species was used at both entrances to unify their identity and reinforce the park's character. Finally, I selected a 12 m-tall specimen as a gateway sentinel in its own right for a significant new district in Reading, UK. This impressive tree sits at the interface of the existing context and the new urban grain introduced by the development. We selected sweetgum for its attention-grabbing presence, which invites people

3

into the space. As I write this, the tree is making its way from mainland Europe and will be in UK soil in time to inspire visitors with its spectacle of color this fall.

One of my favorite spaces in London is the Victoria and Albert Museum's John Madejski Garden, designed by Kim Wilkie. The design includes two standalone *Liquidambars* at the northern corners of the space (fig. 4). The trees stand proudly against the ornate arched facade, and the rich autumn foliage complements the warm vermillion color of the building's stonework. These sweetgums were 7 m tall when planted in 2005 and now exceed 15 m.

4

Trees have the ability to mark personal memories and situate us in a particular place and time as if our neural pathways were entangled with the root system. Like a great melody, a distinct and memorable tree can unearth our deepest memories. One of my favorite song lyrics is in "The Dreaming Tree" by the Dave Matthews Band, which I often reflect on:

> Standing here
> The old man said to me,
> "Long before these crowded streets
> Here stood my dreaming tree"
> Below it he would sit
> For hours at a time
> Now progress takes away what forever
> took to find.

The female flowers of sweetgums produce a diminutive dangling fruit, like dainty, jet-black spiked Christmas baubles silhouetted against a clear sky. Known as *lu lu tong* in China, the sweet gumballs are used for numerous medicinal remedies. Writing about these brings back memories of playful battles I used to have with my wife and kids in a neighborhood play area in Cambridge, Massachusetts. The gumballs had just enough weight to be thrown across the playground, but not enough heft to do any real damage. As a family we would gather as many gumballs as we could hold in the makeshift pouches of our shirts before assuming our positions and unleashing our fury: a fond memory linked to this beautiful tree.

5

As a student working with Ron Henderson, the editor of this compendium, I was tasked with selecting and situating a single species within the Harvard campus. I chose sweetgum and placed it on an elevated landform adjacent to the famous central ramp of Le Corbusier's Carpenter Center for the Visual Arts to allow people to pass the tree at canopy level (fig. 5). My introduction of the sweetgum adds seasonal change and an explosion of color in a fragment of nondescript landscape between Le Corbusier's masterpiece and Renzo Piano's Harvard Art Museums. I can only wonder what Le Corbusier would have thought of my addition to his composition.

Striking winter seedheads
Distinct 'winged' bark growth
February to August
August through November
November to February

Mauritia flexuosa

buriti, moriche palm, ité palm, miriti

Cultivating and Constructing "Brazilianness"

José Tabacow / Florianópolis, Brazil

126

José Tabacow is the director of José Tabacow Landscape Architecture and Environmental Consulting, based in the state of Bahia, Brazil.

1

2

Buriti (*Mauritia flexuosa*) is the most common palm tree in Brazilian landscapes, its range extending throughout the central plateau and the north and northeast of Brazil. In the state of Roraima, in the north of the Amazon region, this species covers practically the entire surface of about 225,000 km², forming extensive colonies and dominating landscapes where water is present (fig. 1). Buriti occupies the

3

humid parts of the Cerrado, Amazon, and Caatinga biomes. In the latter, exclusive to Brazil, it is distributed on a smaller scale due to the long droughts and uncontrolled human exploitation that has drastically reduced the species in northeastern environments. It is almost an aquatic plant, but it also tolerates humid soils in the plains and floodplains along the rivers and streams that cross its native range. These are the so-called gallery forests (along the banks), riparian forests (from the Latin *ripa*, "margin"), or ciliary forests (in the shape of eyelashes). When one of these plants, on the banks or inside a stream, reaches the adult and reproductive stage, its seeds fall into the water and are taken by the current, germinating a little downstream from where the mother plant is. The process reproduces itself successively, creating lines of palm trees in the landscapes that trace the layout of streams and drainage channels. These are *veredas*, the name given by the people of the central plateau to these spectacular groups (fig. 2). Buriti is a species with wide geographical dispersion, extending to other Amazonian countries: the Guianas, Venezuela, Colombia, Peru, Bolivia, and Ecuador. The scientific name of the genus is a tribute to Prince Maurice of Orange, who, in the seventeenth century, came to Brazil to administer a Dutch possession in the tropics. As for the specific name, *flexuosa* means "flexible," perhaps referring to the arches that the petioles form due to their length.

This is one of the most useful of the approximately 450 species of Arecaceae that occur in Brazilian territory. Its fronds, when dry, are used as coverings for houses and small rural facilities, while the rectilinear stipes become columns, posts, and structural parts. From the thousands of scaly fruits, displayed in huge clusters (fig. 3), sweets and ice cream are made. And when the surface of the stems is injured, a sweet gum exudes, which is used to make the prized buriti wine. The main vein of the leaves is used as a paddle and for the structure of rafts and small boats; from the scaly skin of its spherical fruits an essential oil is extracted. As if so many different uses were not enough,

4

5

it is a highly ornamental species, with its large fan-shaped leaves touching in dense clusters that make it a prominent figure in flooded landscapes throughout its geography. It also has the landscape advantage of supporting transplants of any size, depending only on appropriate equipment. In our landscaping design office, we frequently use this species as a way of evoking native landscapes, of making artificial human intervention visually relate to its natural surroundings, while at the same time integrating the landscape design proposal with the scenario where it is inserted. Good examples are Praça dos Cristais (fig. 4) in Brasília and the Ministry of Foreign Affairs (fig. 5) in the same city. In both cases, buritis were collected in their natural environments and transplanted as adults measuring about 7 m in height. The aesthetic results are immediate, the volumes already functioning in the landscapes as dominant elements of the composition and making the visual connection between the human-built landscape and the natural one that is so strongly characterized by this species. Here and there, their gatherings punctuate the landscape where water is present, whether in the form of drains, streams, or rivers, or in the flooding of extensive low-lying areas, which becomes more evident during periods of heavy rain in the region.

Due to its many qualities, landscape architects consider it a charismatic species and use it not only for its aesthetic attributes, but also for the “Brazilianness” that its silhouettes imprint on a large part of the national territory.

Pinus pinea

Italian stone pine

What Is Life as We *Don't* Know It?

Rosetta S. Elkin / New York, USA

Rosetta S. Elkin is a professor and academic director of landscape architecture at the Pratt Institute, a principal of Practice Landscape, and the author of Plant Life. The project described here was funded and supported by the American Academy in Rome and was conducted from February to June 2018.

Why is this plant always—and only—out of reach; disappearing along a perspective line, planted to reflect the temperaments of the city-state? I wanted in. Even if just for a brief moment. Perhaps, I began to imagine, the notoriety of stone pine might help us see our limitations. How could this tree be appreciated for its own sake? I asked myself, what is life as we *don't* know it?

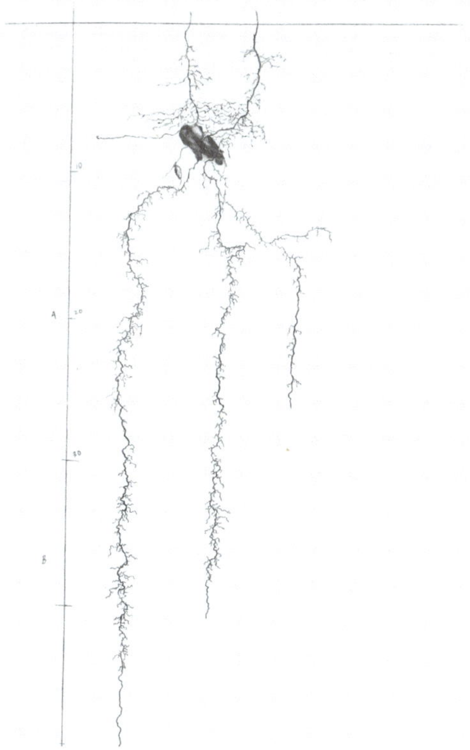

1

2

Italian stone pines are notoriously monumental. Their beauty must be held at a distance, or not at all. Along the streets and parks of Rome, birds pass overhead and shelter within its umbellate canopy, winds emancipate male pollen into yellow clouds, and honey-brown branches slant with the weight of each majestic pinecone. The ecology of *Pinus pinea* progresses while humans watch in amazement from the ground.

It is no wonder that this pine is at once culture and ecology, archaeology and art, enigma and encounter. Its symbolic and spiritual attributes have been known to us since Neolithic cave paintings. Theophrastus describes the aphrodisiac properties of its seed, the sap is recorded as medicine by ancient Romans, and its wood is a staple of early naval construction. Linnaeus named it the "pine of pines." Within the Italian landscape, it is the tree of the painter and the poet. Ovid and Pliny describe it; Virgil and Horace harmonize its ornamental character just as Dante, Decameron, and Botticelli convey its majesty. Still, humans linger on the outside.

When I want to learn more about a plant, I pursue growth, not form. Most often, this draws me into the ground since plant life develops underfoot. I pursued sites where the stone pine was regenerating naturally: less concrete, more soil. Having worked with roots extensively, I also sought a sandy site where excavations were easier, which led me outside the city to Castel Fusano. In my mind, I traveled with two of my heroes for inspiration, the botanist Lore Kutschera and the soil scientist Walter H. Lyford. Kutschera worked up meticulous drawings of single root systems. Lyford coined the term "rhizography" in the field. Taking these together, I aimed to study the development of the stone pine by embracing the complications of the earth—Darwin's tangled bank.

Fieldwork is an exercise in paying attention. The field is my archive, and the ground is a collection that I sift through. The drawings I make are an attempt to share findings in an understandable language. The photographs document the process.

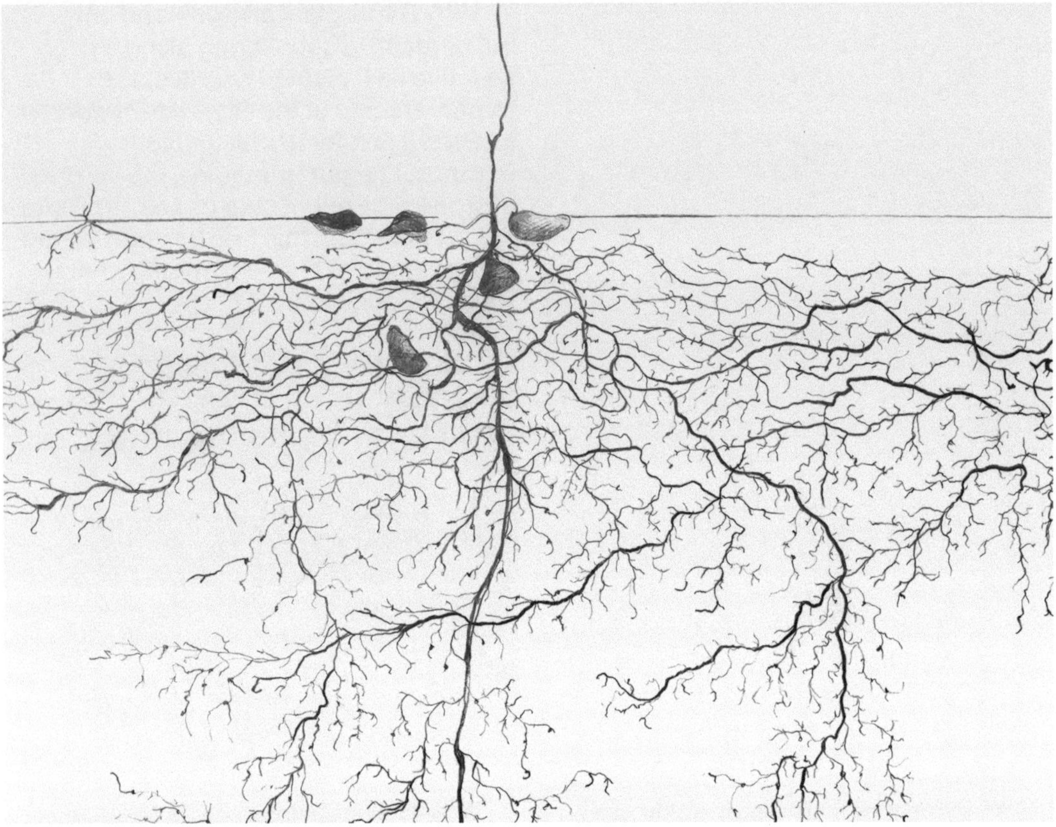

3

My focus was on unearthing seeds. I dug into places with copious pinecones, not fresh ones, but layers that were decomposing and crumbling with age. This was a signal that seeds were dispersed nearby, and I hoped they were nestled in the rhizosphere. A small spade uncovered varying horizons in the soil, and I could feel the temperature of each seed as a register of the landscape. As I tugged on them to see if they were rooted, I felt the pull to a time of ancient trade routes. I felt a pull to a time before the rise of humans, when gymnosperms, plants with naked seeds, prospered because of the free movement of their seed. My mind traveled.

Back at the studio, I marveled at how single seeds preserve enough food to nourish a future sapling and activate the towering pines around me. The seed package has all it needs to encourage root mass, which always emerges from the seed coat first. Once roots are strong enough, the seed invites in the elements and works with other organisms to help it send out a single shoot. I began to draw this process of seeds unfolding, breaking, and foraging. My field sketches and photographs confirmed that some sprouted seeds were typically surrounded by unsprouted or dormant seeds. I imagined them waiting, communicating to one another: you go first. In the library I read about seed behavior. In the field, I recognized they were taking turns, sensing resources to find out which could dive

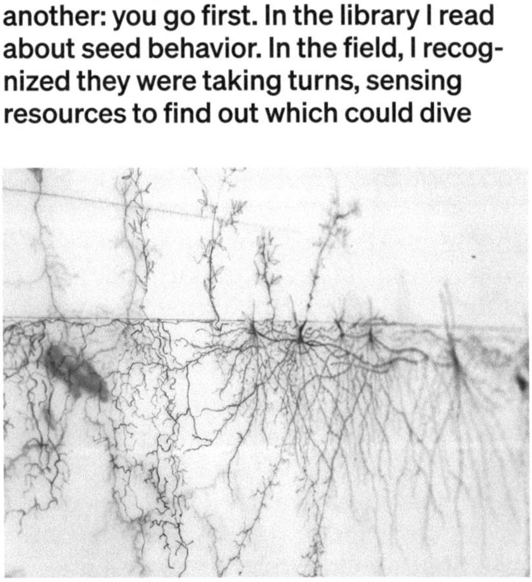

4

deep enough for water while remaining shallow enough to sprout and reach sunlight. They did not compete; they worked together. Dormancy took on new meaning.

The most remarkable interactions occur in the rhizosphere. Woody and nonwoody root systems relate, associate, and signal. Woody root systems are shallow and easy to observe, while fibrous roots are adapted for depth. Imagine a hard-shelled pine nut lodged into a

5

mingled root system, adding its own stems and sources to the framework. Roots forage and fuse. Seeds are part of the consortium. Such seeds remain durable for years in the ground, just as they might on your shelf. Both hold the capacity to germinate for longer than scientists understand. We still can't get close enough.

One of the most meaningful ways to advance planting design in landscape architecture is to discover how plants *grow*, a paradigm shift in a field that is absorbed with classification and identification that can only describe how plants *look*. Perhaps it is time again, to start from seed.

Pinus thunbergii

Japanese black pine, matsu-zukuri

Shaping and Being Shaped

Aki Omi / San Francisco, USA, and Tokyo, Japan

136

Aki Omi is a landscape architect and founder of office ma.

The tree. Black pines are quintessential elements of Japanese landscapes, gardens, and art: ukiyo-e by Hokusai and Hiroshige, Noh theater backdrops, kimonos (fig. 1). In traditional Japanese gardens, they are used to evoke the ideal of mountainous or coastal landscapes.

The beach. At Suma Beach, tenacious trunks of black pines emerge from bare ground, writhing in unique shapes created by strong coastal winds. Seemingly in a natural state, they were likely planted—perhaps by the shogunate—two hundred years ago as part of a campaign to line new roads and protect the coast from erosion. I still remember the precise steps I took through the forest, as a child from landlocked Nara, to get to the beach when my family would visit my uncle in Shioya, a small village in Kobe, where Suma Beach beckoned (figs. 2 and 3). As a port town, Kobe also had a Western presence, including a neighborhood of Westerners called James Hill that occupied a bluff above Suma Beach. There, over my teenaged summers, I became exposed to ideas and culture from outside Japan.

1

The house. My father planted a black pine, a *matsu-zukuri*, next to the gate in front of our house in Nara. He spent many hours over many years training its branches into a perfect arch to welcome guests. This tree became an iconic part of our house, forever intermingled with the identity of my father. The form he gave to this pine was very different from the pines I saw at the beach, yet no less idealized. The pine's many forms all reflect a push and pull between the tree's inner nature and the will of external forces, be they the wind or my father (fig. 4).

The journey. At the age of sixteen, rebelling against the same cultural forces shaping me that were employed to shape the Japanese black pine, I set out alone to America as an exchange student—with the full support of my dad, who managed to have my name removed from the high school rolls, making it virtually impossible to return to school in Japan. He perhaps understood me as he understood his black pine arching over the garden gate. Life in Japan is lived with forces of shaping and being shaped.

America provided the freedom to shape myself. A guidance counselor at Georgia Southern University, who assumed things about me because she had Japanese friends who had a Japanese garden, first suggested the

2

3

idea of landscape architecture. I was tentatively testing my options when I enrolled at Ohio State University with a triple major of business, premed, and landscape architecture. As my undergraduate term ended, I followed advice from a partner at the design firm Sasaki, who recommended that I move to Boston, where I began my career in landscape architecture in the Cambridge office of George Hargreaves and earned my master's in landscape architecture at Harvard, culminating with my own firm, office ma, which now practices in both North America and Asia.

4

The return. Until my return to Japan, I would have avoided using black pines, along with other predictable components of traditional Japanese gardens. Earlier in my career, I found the assumption that I do Japanese gardens unsettling. However, I am exploring some of these components now as my work seeks to coerce abstractions from something already as abstract as a Japanese garden.

One landscape that helped clarify this exploration of abstraction—one that I came to know later in my career as a landscape architect—is the two thousand black pines arrayed across a rigorously flat ground plane at the Imperial Palace in Tokyo, planted some eighty years ago. I experienced this monocultural black pine landscape often as I traveled to Tokyo during the design and construction of office ma's Otemachi One Garden across the street from the palace grounds. Those black pines remind me of the childhood beach at Suma with their contorted trunks casting shadows across the ground—and they evoke powerful memories of my father. No two of these black pines are alike, though they undergo careful candling twice a year by master gardeners who work to express the inner form of each tree (fig. 5).

We recently completed a project in Tokyo's Toyosu neighborhood, where we planted six hundred trees as a windbreak required by government regulations.

6

5

Toyosu is a flat, waterfront landfill created from debris from the 1923 earthquake as a staging ground for the rebuilding of the city. A portion of the new landscape traces the wind, creating a corridor of sculpted landforms and forest canopy. Inspired by my childhood memory of Kobe, and like the shogunate before, we selected black pines to reinforce the coastal landscape, and we curated a collection of trees with unique individual forms. With no intention of shaping them by hand, we will allow the wind to shape them over time (fig. 6).

In Japanese, the syllables *matsu* mean both "pine" and "waiting." It is a fitting linguistic twist for the black pine, which takes its form in response to natural forces enacted over centuries—as well as patient and dedicated human manipulation. Time will tell.

Death. My father was tragically killed by a drunken hit-and-run driver in 2003. I owe much to my father, who recognized in me, as he did in his prized black pine gateway, an innate potential, individual will, and drive toward perfection.

Platanus ×acerifolia

London planetree

The Ubiquitous Urban Champion

Gary Hilderbrand / Cambridge, USA

Gary Hilderbrand is a landscape architect and founding principal of Reed Hilderbrand. He is the Peter Louis Hornbeck professor in practice of landscape architecture and chair of the Landscape Architecture Department at the Harvard Graduate School of Design.

I love the London planetree, or plane for short, for two reasons. The first is the tree itself—a majestic, muscular aristocrat of great beauty. The second is its ubiquity in cities that thrived and expanded in the nineteenth century; cities around the world made the choice to feature the plane along boulevards and highways in vast numbers (fig. 1). Many of these survive today. These kinds of plantations helped forge a modern space of travel, beauty, and utility in cities.

This great friend is a cross between two morphologically distinct species: the Oriental plane (*Platanus orientalis*) and the American sycamore (*Platanus occidentalis*). It is believed that the cross originated in the seventeenth century in London, though definitive proof is lacking. It appeared in large numbers in London and Spain by the eighteenth century. Today, the tree is grown in northern Europe, the US, China, South America, and elsewhere as part of urban

1

infrastructure: half of all the trees in London are planes, 43 percent of all the trees in Paris, 15 percent of the street trees in New York City. Nanjing and Shanghai have the largest numbers of planes; French occupation made this so.

The London plane is strikingly large, with a stout trunk and upright, spreading stems (fig. 2). Structurally, this is among the strongest beings on earth. In age, its canopy spread can reach 20–30 m and occasionally much more. Its height typically

2

3

4

reaches 30 m (fig. 3). Its leaves, which are deciduous, are outsized, nearly the largest among our northern hardwoods: 20–25 cm across, usually with three to five lobes. The leaves exhibit transparency in bright light and opacity when the light is soft. It presents male and female flowers in separate clusters on the same tree—one of the keys to its survival and proliferation. It thrives in moist bottomland soils but also does well in the upland, which experiences frequent drought and extreme high temperatures. It suffers few pests save a menacing fungus that is thankfully rare—canker stain—and another, anthracnose, that is common and sometimes disfiguring but not fatal.

One other remarkable and defining trait: a tolerance for lousy soil and harmful surface conditions. You can pave entirely around this tree with basalt rock or asphalt, park a street sweeper on its roots, or plow a speeding Mini Cooper into it, which is known to produce extensive damage to the vehicle. This is never the fault of the tree. The planetree is, beyond measure, a good citizen in the city.

It may have first been observed in the early industrial city of London that the plane had developed specific adaptations that allowed it to survive the hazardous conditions of the Victorian street: ever-present soot in the air, manure and wretched fluids on the pavement, contamination in the soil, and constant injury from collisions with its trunk. While these adaptations are not in themselves responses to urbanization—they're evolutionary adaptive traits—they've enabled the plane to survive the toughest urban conditions.

Perhaps the most productive adaptations are those of the root structure to compaction and salinity. Trees don't survive our urban conditions without these traits. Furthermore, the plane is radically heliotropic: if they need to, the tree's branches forcefully bend towards the sun. In one of my favorite instances, on the streets that line the Tiber River in Rome, you can see the highly improbable condition of branches reaching into a space physically lower than the root mass of the tree (fig. 4). The bright reflected light from the high walls of the river embankment helps the tree to produce more canopy as a response to difficult growing conditions. This also results from a pruning regime called coppicing, where multiple leaders are pruned hard in youth to produce three or four codominant stems that will grow straight towards the sky. These trees work exceedingly well in the narrow space of the embankment roadway. If the tree cannot produce on one side of its crown, it will always compensate on the other, more open side.

Another adaptation, which is extremely rare among hardwoods, is the renewal of bark tissue by exfoliation. This molting, which gives rise to the mottling of color and texture that so strongly attracts me to this tree, heals injuries and rids the bark of particulates and foreign substances (fig. 5). And here is the very unique thing:

5

if the tree loses its leaf cover to some possible calamity, this molting bark is able to participate in photosynthesis so that nutrient exchange can be sustained. Green bark—a very useful adaptation for a tree that withstands regular urban tortures (fig. 6).

I can only lament that city arborists tend to reject the London plane today due to its ubiquity, in the name of biodiversity. So, while I have planted many hundreds of trees over the years, I've never planted the one I love the most. But I don't need to travel very far to see it. It's everywhere.

6

Plinia cauliflora

jabuticabeira

Joyful Sensory Pleasures

Lucia Maria Sá Antunes Costa / Rio de Janeiro, Brazil

Lucia Maria Sá Antunes Costa is a professor of landscape architecture in the Programa de Pós-Graduação em Urbanismo at the Universidade Federal do Rio de Janeiro.

Brazil is a country that holds one of the greatest varieties of native trees. Among them, fruit trees represent a remarkable collection, found in all Brazilian biomes. Many of them were taken to other countries and adapted very well around the world. Others, however, do not easily adapt far from their original biome—which is the case with the jabuticabeira, one of my favorite ones.

1

Native to the Atlantic Forest biome, it occurs mainly in the Brazilian southeast states of Minas Gerais, São Paulo, and Rio de Janeiro. The name of its fruit, jabuticaba, is of Tupi-Guarani origin, and translates as "fruits in bud." It is a fruit tree that has been cultivated since the nineteenth century, both on large farms and in private residential backyards. Jabuticaba is very popular and is featured in Brazilian cuisine, literature, poetry, feasts, and other cultural manifestations.

And what makes the jabuticabeira so special?

It is a large tree, 9–10 m in height, having a low trunk, small green leaves, and thin branches that open in forks towards the sky (fig. 1). It is a spectacle during the flowering and fruiting season. As if in a sudden explosive moment of beauty, all its branches turn completely white, covered with tiny little flowers glued to each other. The flowers attract small bees that, with their buzzing, bring an unmistakable melody to the jabuticabeira. Approximately forty days after flowering, the fruits begin to form, the beauty of their changing colors alluring as they grow: initially green, gradually darkening to purple, and finally reaching a shiny black tone when they are ripe—turning the branches, to which they cling tightly, from white to black (fig. 2). The peculiar way they go from white to green to purple to black sets the rhythm of time in this unique tree.

The jabuticabeira invites us to pick and taste its fruits in a particular way that requires understanding of the tree's structure—to figure out the best way to get inside it, find a way through the labyrinth of its branches, and get "in" the tree. Then another rhythm begins: picking the fruit, biting into its thick black skin, feeling the juiciness and sweetness of its white pulp, and then spitting out its dark seed. This experience is never a lonely one. With jabuticabas, many other insects and birds, such as wasps and parakeets, arrive to join the small bees that come to pierce the fruits with their stingers or beaks to taste its pulp. When we are literally inside the jabuticabeira eating its fruits, we enjoy a remarkable experience, like a symphony, of humming and singing (fig. 3).

2

The fruiting of the jabuticabeira is plentiful, but fast and brief. All of us—humans and animals—have about one week to pick and taste the hundreds of fruits offered by a single tree, since they quickly go sour. Jabuticaba, due to its abundance, is a fruit to be shared, and in the countryside, many farms welcome people to pick and consume their fruits on the spot, though not to take them home. Likewise, in the urban backyards and orchards of small towns in the countryside, neighbors and friends are invited to come in and enjoy the fruits (fig. 4).

Over more than two hundred years, the jabuticabeira has been mostly cultivated in private spaces. On farms, it was commonly planted as an orchard unto itself or mixed with other fruit trees. Residents of small towns also planted their jabuticabeiras in orchards or backyards. It was not usual to see this tree planted in ornamental gardens or parks and squares.

In recent years jabuticabeiras have played a greater role in the practice of landscape architecture. Over the last decades, many Brazilian landscape architects have designed their private and public gardens to reflect the value they place on the uniqueness of this remarkable tree (fig. 5). Luciano Fiaschi, a landscape architect in São Paulo, has included these trees in the design of residential front gardens and on properties of different scales—in rows or as a landmark specimen, in order to bring a special atmosphere to a particular place. Landscape architects have been exploring jabuticabeiras for their possibilities as landscape space-makers as well as the unique flowering and fruiting experience they offer.

We know that values and meanings for trees always change across time. Celebrating the joy and sensory pleasures of a fruit tree, such as the jabuticabeira, is a landscape architect's expression of Brazilian culture as well as a revelation of a deep connection with nature.

3
4

Lorenzi, H. 1988. *Árvores brasileiras: Manual de identificação e cultivo de plantas arbóreas nativas do Brasil*. Nova Odessa: Plantarum.

Raseira, M. do C. B., L. E. C. Antunes, R. Trevisan, and E. D. Gonçalves, eds. 2014. *Espécies frutíferas do sul do Brasil*. Pelotas: EMBRAPA.

5

Plinia cauliflora

Populus alba

white poplar, silver poplar, sepidar

The Striking White Columnar Silhouette of Human Settlements

Morteza Adib and Maryam Yousefi / Tehran, Iran

Morteza Adib is a landscape architect and architect in Tehran, where he is an assistant professor at Shahid Beheshti University. He and Maryam Yousefi, also a landscape architect and architect, are the founders of Contextlogic Architects, also based in Tehran.

1

White poplars—*abes* or *sepidar* in Persian—are a common sight throughout Iran, where their columnar trunks covered in bright white bark punctuate the silhouettes of villages, towns, and gardens (fig. 2). They are often closely planted as windbreaks, their tall wall of foliage bravely facing the forces of nature. When planted in a row, they create a striking line that marches across open landscapes, such as the row of poplars by the Epte River that inspired the French impressionist painter Claude Monet (1840–1926) to create a series of paintings that capture their elongated white trunks and fluttering foliage in changeable seasonal and atmospheric conditions: in the evening, in the sun, on a windy day, in gray weather, at the end of autumn (fig. 1).

Their vertical, symmetrical habit creates spaces and visual emphases that are memorable landscapes in many cultures. The leaves have a velvety texture with a dark green upper surface and a dusty white underside, the contrast between which adds chromatic depth and fluttering light to the landscape. Additionally, these trees provide a habitat for a variety of birds and other wildlife, making them an important part of the ecosystem.

Despite their many attributes, there are also downsides to consider when planting white poplars, including their relatively short lifespan (typically twenty to thirty years) and the significant amounts of water they require, which can be a concern in areas where water is scarce. Additionally, their roots can cause damage to building

3

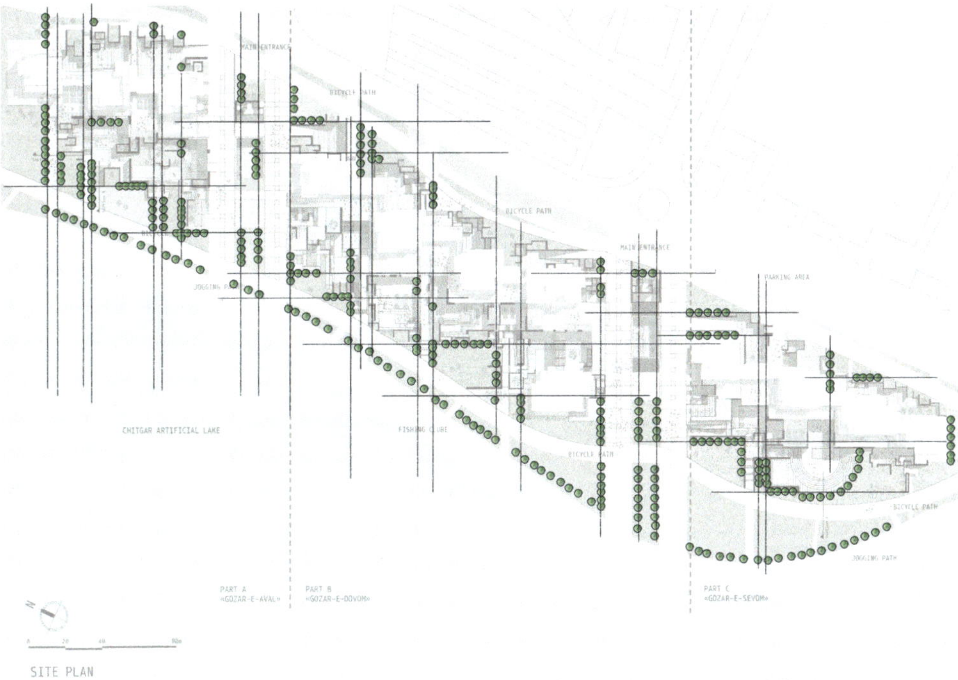
MAIN ENTRANCE
BICYCLE PATH
BICYCLE PATH
MAIN ENTRANCE
PARKING AREA
CHITGAR ARTIFICIAL LAKE
BICYCLE PATH
BICYCLE PATH
JOGGING PATH
PART A
«GOZAR-E-AVAL»
PART B
«GOZAR-E-DOVOM»
PART C
«GOZAR-E-SEVOM»
SITE PLAN

2

4

foundations, sidewalks, and other structures. Despite these limitations, white poplars are still highly valued for their use in landscape architecture.

The garden courtyards and landscape of the Bamland recreational complex began with a proposal to construct a 25,000 m² retail center on 5 ha of land along the eastern bank of Chitgar Lake in Tehran. The original plan consisted of a conventional commercial building surrounded by green spaces. However, given the expansive size of the site and its prime location by the reservoir, the question was raised: "How can we elevate the landscape and foster an urban atmosphere in conjunction with the commercial building?" To answer this question, we worked to reconfigure the project with an emphasis on "in-between spaces," the ambiguous zone between architecture and landscape that acts as a liminal space for vibrant urban life.

The design program underwent significant changes to achieve a landscape that infiltrates the buildings with parallel rows of white poplars amidst a series of connected courtyards (fig. 3). The aboveground building density was reduced, the mass was divided, and the land was terraced. Trees and gardens were integrated into these "in-between spaces," with low-rise symmetry reminiscent of the settings and proportions of historical Persian dwellings.

The tree's presence, varying in levels and heights, provides a sense of familiarity and comfort for visitors, recalling rural or garden landscapes, where its fast growth rate and straight trunks make it valuable for farm fences and poles. At Bamland, the growth rate of these trees in the lake's microclimate, which is more humid than that of Tehran, has exceeded expectations, adding maturity to the landscape within just five years since planting. The white poplars also mark narrow pathways between the project's landscape and the lake paths—meandering like Monet's poplars along the shore. The tree's tall and upright form, arranged in multiple rows that form canopy masses, also transforms the linked sequence of courtyards into shaded groves (fig. 4) enclosed by the trees' striking white bark, with its characteristic dark diamond-shaped fissures.

While the canopy silhouette structures the skyline, the space under the poplars is also captivating (fig. 5). Coupled with the dappled shadows cast on the ground and the duotone leaves, white poplars create speckled patterns of white, black, and green that reverberate in the landscape. In the sunlight, spaces beneath white poplars shimmer: the fluttering shadows of trees that reach for the sky.

5

Populus deltoides

eastern cottonwood

Codesign with a Cottony Collaborator

Sean Burkholder / Philadelphia, USA

Sean Burkholder is an assistant professor of landscape architecture at the University of Pennsylvania's Weitzman School of Design and a founding partner of the research and design practice PROOF Projects.

In North America, the eastern cottonwood is a polarizing character. Like so many quickly established plants, its rambunctious qualities tend to be the characteristic dividing its fans and critics. Cottonwoods are the fastest-growing hardwood tree in the United States, easily achieving 150 cm per year. They spread quickly by way of seed or vegetal parts, particularly along waterways and coastlines. In many ways, these qualities *should* tether them more temporally to us humans, as you could essentially watch a tuft of seed hit the ground in the morning, find the tree it produces shading your house in the afternoon, and then watch it drop branches on your car before bedtime. But instead, these characteristics deter the planting of cottonwood—with its richly furrowed, fingerprint-like bark—in human environments where stability and predictability are desired, and it is often relegated to sacrificial applications associated with restoration and remediation (fig. 1).

1

As a formidable character in the precolonial landscape of North America, cottonwood was the subject of many indigenous stories. It is said that the five-pointed stars that can be found in the cut branches of the tree were traveling from the earth to the night sky up through the cottonwood tree. It was also used by settlers for everything from chicken coops to coffins, and as a quick-growing shade tree.

For all its attributes, the eastern cottonwood is downright abhorred by many. It is difficult to find an arboretum or botanical-garden publication that has anything nice to say about it. Based on how much complaining is done, it seems that most do not see much application for the cottonwood in the designed landscape; even its wood is only good for pulp and pallets. Of course, Frederick Law Olmsted (1822–1903) used cottonwood to vegetate the sewerage landscape of Boston's Back Bay Fens, and it gets smeared all over the top of landfills for remediation purposes—such as the Clearview Landfill remediation in Philadelphia, where cottonwoods and hybrid poplars were used (fig. 2). When it comes to a city tree, the cottonwood is seen as unreliable at best, and, after an initial spate of popularity, it gave way to more sensible elm, ash, maple, and honey locust. All this said, the cottonwood can have a place in the designed landscape; it will just require a different mindset with regard to the process of planting design.

The most useful method of utilizing cottonwood is to leverage what it already does well—growing and spreading. Look around unmanaged riverine or lacustrine landscapes and you are likely to find cottonwoods. A small pathway across a dike at Ken Euers Nature Area in Green Bay, Wisconsin, exhibits this beautifully. Cottonwoods have established themselves on both sides of the path to create an allée that would be difficult to make better if you tried (fig. 3). Here, the proximity of the body to chattering leaves and deeply rutted bark captures just how experientially powerful the tree can be. At nearby Cat Island, thousands of volunteer cottonwood saplings flutter on the surface of recently placed muddy dredged sediment (fig. 4). You can almost sit and watch them grow. Through acts of encouragement and discouragement—or better yet, *collaboration*—you do not need to *plant* cottonwoods; instead, plan for them to show up unannounced, just like your family during the holidays, and figure out what to do with them when they do.

2

3

At Silo City in Buffalo, New York, I "collaborated" with cottonwoods that were already growing sporadically along the drainage channel of an abandoned railroad track. By turning this track into a pedestrian path and digging out the channel, the spatial experience of a long arching trail lined by fluttering leaves *happened*—practically on its own. This trail terminates at a majestic old cottonwood (the likely source of all the progeny), complete with tree swing (fig. 5).

I argue that we need more of this kind of planting, where we work with what is already there or will show up on its own. Instead of imposing our abstract vegetal expectations—expectations that often require a lot of work to keep intact—let us embrace the unruly workings of the world around us and leverage the formative and experiential possibilities of what is already happening. Most likely, there will always be cottonwood there somewhere. Long live the (short-lived) cottonwood!

4 

5 

Populus nigra var. *italica*

Lombardy poplar

A Green Ideal for Santiago, Chile

Romy Hecht / Santiago de Chile, Chile

Romy Hecht is an architect, a professor of the history and theory of landscape architecture, and the head of College UC at Pontificia Universidad Católica de Chile.

Chile is an almost invisible strip of land, 4,720 km long and 180 km wide between the snowcapped Andes Mountains and the Pacific Ocean, that evolved as an isolated backwater—initially at the margins of the Incan empire and then of Spanish colonization. Just as the territory was an interlude in European expeditions of political and economic expansion until well into the eighteenth century, Chile's capital city was no more than an outpost in bioprospecting journeys to procure valuable foreign botanicals for acclimatization and collection.

1

Founded in a relatively flat basin characterized by a dry atmosphere and daily temperature contrasts, Santiago did not offer a natural scenario for a variety of plants. Since rain falls only in winter, cacti, thorny shrubs, and the espino (*Vachellia caven*, a tree that rarely exceeds 6 m in height), prevailed in nonirrigated fields. From the nineteenth century onwards, however, exotic tree-planting systems were envisioned as malleable agents of urban reform and modernization, displaying a connection between utility, beauty, sustenance, and the representation of an independent nation.

In this scenario grew Lombardy poplars, their rapid growth even in poor soils, ease of transplanting (cuttings taken from hardwood stems can be placed directly in their final setting), and resistance to violent pruning making them suitable candidates for quickly providing Santiago with a monumental, dark, and thriving green foliage.

Although the Jesuits brought poplars, or álamos, to Chile during colonial times, their use as urban trademarks only began in January 1810, when the Franciscan priest José Javier de Guzmán (1759–1840) succeeded with the first public planting of Lombardy poplars in the country. Using nineteen year-old sapling scions that had survived the trip from Mendoza, Argentina, he enhanced the facade of his church and convent in La Cañada, and with it, the eroded condition of Santiago's main and widest road.

In 1817, the supreme director of the newly established Republic of Chile, Bernardo O'Higgins (1778–1842), built on

Alamedas in Santiago by the 1830s, from T. R. Harvey, Panorama of Santiago from the Santa Lucía Hill, View towards the West/North (1860)

Guzmán's initial work. Along 11 km, he profusely planted the trees close enough to shape a tall tunnel, an alameda, whose straightness, solemn physiognomy, and colors of intense green, light gray, and bright gold stood out in stark contrast to the city's horizontality and persistent harsh colonial guise (fig. 1).

Under O'Higgins's rule, La Cañada became the Alameda de las Delicias, a promenade combining two double and triple rows of Lombardy poplars on either side of cobblestoned irrigation ditches, or acequias, which kept the rubbish out of sight and lessened the odors it could carry while still conveying water to the trees. O'Higgins also introduced scrupulous maintenance of his planted *plaisirs*: while reducing stormwater runoff, properly pruned poplars became sculptural masses structuring a striking shaded walkway that offered comfort, recreation, and delight to the people, the same unstoppable *populus* with which the species' Latin name is so strongly associated due to its fluttering leaves, easily set in motion by the slightest breeze.

As Santiago's first designed landscape, the Alameda de las Delicias also provided all the necessary saplings and stocks to shape other poplar-lined avenues. By the 1830s, the construction and maintenance of alamedas would be at the heart of the city's expansion efforts, which resulted in a new skyline defined by a visually striking green foliage that in time became a symbol of the city (figs. 2 and 3).

3

Avenida de las Delicias, View of the Promenade (c. 1920), from Hume & Walker, Souvenir of Santiago

2

4

As infrastructure to support agricultural production, álamos acquired an additional value in Santiago's rural outskirts. Planted in long winding rows, they outlined watercourses for irrigation and access roads to properties while serving as windbreaks for crops, making possible the conversion of a semiarid territory into a fertile, prosperous, and particularly renowned winegrowing valley.

In time, Lombardy poplars also demonstrated the discrepancy between appearance and purpose in landscape practices: their shallow roots broke through road surfaces, calling into question their functional suitability for roadside planting and highlighting the need to expand and diversify Santiago's botanical collection. Direct consequences were the slow transformation of the city's landscapes into a hybrid of newly imported landscape repertoires and the introduction of tree diversity, to the point that, nowadays, more than 90 percent of tree species are exotic to the country.

Today Lombardy poplars are hardly seen in Chile's capital city, but their massive presence throughout the country—in places like Rancagua and Lonquimay-Malalcahuello—reminds us that the first thriving public urban trees impacted the process of nation-making by providing a collective identity to Chile's capital city through an ensemble of exotic trees and geometries of planting where there had been none (figs. 4 and 5).

5

Psidium friedrichsthalianum

Costa Rican guava, cas

Patterns of Common Language

José Vargas Hidalgo and Dana Víquez Azofeifa / San José, Costa Rica

José Vargas Hidalgo and Dana Víquez Azofeifa are founding partners at PPAR, a studio for landscape and architecture based in San José, Costa Rica.

1

Every patio in Costa Rica used to have a cas.

A patio is primarily a backyard, although it also includes front yards. This dualism explains the totality of the landscape contained in a household. In Costa Rica, a patio can take many forms and connect various areas, thereby relating programmatic uses.

The patio can be described as a unit of landscape, the extent of space in which residents can modify, transform, and experiment with landscape. As urbanization grows, patios become the resistance of landscape, stains for the survival of flora and fauna. Even when divided by property lines, patios communicate with each other: for example, it is known that underground bioconnectivity is essential for trees to share information and nutrients, and therefore to thrive, all as a system.

It is within these systems that a peculiar tree catches our attention. The idea of choosing the cas tree begins with the curiosity to explore what one can consider an allusion to good practices: a cas was always there, carelessly growing as a centerpiece of our homes (fig. 1).

A cas is a fruit tree; however, it is not our intention to promote the use of fruit-bearing trees in all city spaces, as they can be very demanding in terms of maintenance. On the other hand, we must recognize that fruit trees can be a good reason for a walk and social interaction when found in parks and public spaces (fig. 2).

Instead, we are interested in pointing out a tree that could represent both a cultural and a biological reference, in pointing out the way these species tell the story of a landscape that gives continuity to material culture, its input to endemic landscapes, and the role of landscape architects in the formation of collective languages within a region. Rather than providing a dendrological description of our subject, we aim to convey a conceptual assembly of how a tree can become a pattern of common understanding.

The ground around a cas is covered with fallen fruit mixed with pistils, petals, and strips of bark, extending to the entire perimeter. Our tree brings out shadows and patchy fragments of the light behind it; its dense foliage allows glimpses of the sky behind.

2

One can climb it; we did as kids to pick fruit. Its strong branches are flexible enough to hold swings and make the most precise slingshots. Its trunk is sculptural, solid, and sometimes curvy, depending on the neighboring trees and the space around it. Its smooth texture makes it attractive for tactile discovery. It camouflages, varying from light beige to areas of green and brown depending on its geometry.

Even though its silhouette is very recognizable, what stands out is the fruit. The cas produces a small round fruit between 3 and 7 cm in diameter. Its insides are white, and a small cluster of edible seeds can be found in the interior. These seeds are small enough to be swallowed and hard enough to break a tooth. But most importantly, the flavor: an unexpected combination of sour and sweet, hard and soft; a mouth-watering fragrance. A cas can awaken slumbering memories, spatial and sensory (fig. 3).

These qualities are not enough. The place of actuation of these units of landscape, where the cas is found, is shifting. The impact of rapid urbanization and uncontrollable infrastructures force these landscapes to be transferred to other formats. As we now live in smaller spaces, our buildings have no room for planting.

3

Nature is now somewhere else: rivers, parks, boulevards, and at best, some streets. These are everyone's front yards and backyards.

The inclusion of these remnants of landscape found in a city's spaces can contribute to broader natural circuits of exchange. This is a system of connectivity for the survival, feeding, and reproduction of animals as well. For what are now considered "urban species"—some birds, sloths, insects, and amphibians—are intrinsically dependent on the continuity of these landscape units (fig. 4).

As cities demand better urban environments with larger and denser green spaces, new generations are to be encouraged to experience nature; the

evidence of this is the surge of civil and governmental initiatives to rehabilitate and amplify green space and the way we interact with it.

The landscape architect's task of systematizing and preserving is extended to the task of identifying this transference of vegetative materials, performance, and aesthetics. Hence, the task is also to locate and pursue possible cultural continuity through nature.

In the end, every house still has a cas tree, and the urge to experience landscape persists. We encourage the use of recognizable species—culturally rooted, functional, and inscribed in the imaginary: here is where beauty proliferates.

4

Quercus agrifolia

coast live oak, yuukiš, yuukš, bellota de encino

The Patient Giant

Story Wiggins / San Francisco, USA

Story Wiggins is a landscape architect with a background in historic preservation and land stewardship. She is a partner at Terremoto.

I am a newcomer to the West by any measure. Though in modern Bay time, ten years seems positively rooted, it is orders of magnitude less than the maybe ten thousand years the Ohlone people have spent on this land, and has nothing on the twenty million during which the coast live oak has ebbed and flowed along the California coast. Despite my transplant status, I felt an immediate kinship to this ubiquitous giant tree (fig. 1).

for this reason we often include them in our planting palettes. Though they feel relatively common in the landscape, 90 percent of precolonial oak woodland has been lost to development. Not to mention the break in the indigenous land-management practices—controlled burns, most notably—that kept those ecosystems in balance and raging wildfires at bay. So it never feels superfluous or tired to plant them.

1

Familiar, its enveloping and spreading quality reminded me of the moss-draped southern live oaks (*Quercus virginiana*) of my youth in South Carolina. And it had something of the stately grace of the beech trees I knew and loved in Rhode Island, of which it is a distant relative. But despite these affinities, the coast live oak seems distinctly more aloof, unbothered and unfussy, more rugged and open-ended: a tree fit for the West (fig. 2).

At Terremoto, practically every rural project site we visit is punctuated by pauses of awe under these venerable trees. They look right and do well almost anywhere west of the Central Valley, and

Sometimes that's tucked close together as a screening hedge, which over time urges them to grow tall and thin, creating a spooky understory of dancing trunks and filtered light (fig. 3). Occasionally, in an act of gentle subterfuge, we sneak tiny saplings into planting areas unbeknownst to the client—by the time they're large enough to require a second thought we'll all be long gone. Often it's as a feature tree for the future, because even the largest box trees lack the gravitas of the specimens that have been standing in the landscape for a century or more. On many projects, our most significant act is to protect and care for the sentient elders

2

3

that already exist on the site. This too is an act of design.

Our friends Vincent Medina (of the Chochenyo Ohlone) and Louis Trevino (Rumsen Ohlone) see the coast live oak as a defining feature of their homeland in the East Bay. When we worked with them to design a dining and education space for their cultural organization and restaurant, mak-'amham, they chose another native oak, the valley oak (*Quercus lobata*), as the focal point and sentinel of the garden because its acorns are a primary ingredient in their cooking. But they appreciate the rough and resilient qualities of the coast live oak as an omnipresent link between generations of their people. They know the coast live oak as yuukiš in the Chochenyo dialect, yuukš in Rumsen, or bellota de encino in the old California Spanish dialect also spoken by their family. They know that the vast forests of coast live oak that their ancestors stewarded gave Oakland its name.

4

Though their acorns are less desirable for humans, they are a staple for many birds and small mammals, which help to cultivate new groves through their occasional forgetfulness. The tree is a keystone species of sunlit oak-woodland habitats, where they serve as a likely host plant for over a hundred butterfly and moth species, as cover and habitat for vertebrates large and small, and in relationship with innumerable microscopic and underground beings. Masters of their own destiny and domain, these oaks will not tolerate fertilization or summer water, preferring instead to maintain the closed-loop system of composition and decomposition that cycles from their leaves to their roots and in the soil at their feet.

This year, 2023, more than any in my memory, the oaks are blooming with abandon. Bright green catkins sprout and droop from the tips of branches in celebration of the rain that has lashed our coast this winter. Despite this display, and all of their resilient adaptations, these ancient creatures are not immune to the atmospheric changes we have triggered. Sudden oak death, a disease as bad as it sounds, caused by the pathogen *Phytophthora ramorum*, spreads more easily in wet winters, especially to drought-stressed trees. There is a camp in the native-plant community that advises against planting them at all anymore. In humble, optimistic resistance, we forge on, with careful sourcing and contextual sensitivity, to plant the next generation (fig. 4).

Planting a coast live oak is an offering to the future and to the more-than-human world, connecting us all across time in a way that feels essential now. A 95 L container tree will remain scrubby for twenty years before beginning to stretch out into its cathedralesque apotheosis (fig. 5). This yielding to delayed gratification is a ritual of going slowly, of patience, of letting go. More and more, we seek to build these gifts into our gardens, allowing the timescale of the seasons, plants, animals, and rocks to act as friction and ballast against the slippery, perpetual illusion of now we all inhabit.

5

Quercus deserticola

encino chaparro, encino del pedregal, encino texmole

Ecosystem Builder for Geological Times

Pedro Camarena Berruecos /
Mexico City, Mexico

Pedro Camarena Berruecos is a landscape architect and a faculty member at the School of Landscape Architecture in the Universidad Nacional Autónoma de México's College of Architecture. He is the International Federation of Landscape Architects' chair of professional practice and policy for the Americas region.

Translated from the Spanish by Alexis Arias Betancourt.

1

In Mexico, the genus *Quercus* is widely represented. Of five hundred species known worldwide, various authors state that three hundred exist in our country, and eighty-six of them are endemic to Mexico. In their article "Encinos de México," Silvia Romero Rangel and her coauthors (2015, 74–75) state that

2

3

4

"specialists consider Mexico to be the epicenter of diversification of the genus since it is the country with the highest number of species of this genus."

During the Spanish conquest, the use of oak in construction and as an energy source (mostly charcoal) was prevalent. Consequently, the *Quercus* communities dwelling on the slopes and mountains surrounding the Mexico basin declined substantially, and their slow growth rate precluded consideration as a species for forest management. In the early twenty-first century, there is a growing interest in their production for forest management and for planting in urban areas. However, except for a few producers in the country's northern region (specifically in the state of Nuevo León), it is challenging to find oak specimens suitable for use in urban landscape projects.

Among the oak species that are being considered more frequently is encino texmole (*Quercus deserticola*), due to its resistance to extreme conditions—poor soil, scarce water, and high solar exposure. This tree inhabits the rocky areas of the Pedregal lava fields south of Mexico City, where it was "trapped" on the Cerro Zacatépetl when it was surrounded by lava from the eruption of the volcano Xitle almost 1,700 years ago (fig. 1). In mythology, this is the hill where Huitzilopochtli, the patron of the Mexica people, was conceived. The rivers of magma swept away every living being in their path, leaving the hilltop encino texmole to colonize the lava fields when the incandescent rock cooled down.

The species had to evolve rapidly as a resilient tree able to thrive in these adverse conditions, and it was a crucial pioneer for a new ecosystem in constant ecological succession. It is an ecosystem builder (fig. 2). We should consider this resilience in relation to the contemporary conditions imposed by climate change, which require us to carefully select plants that can withstand various meteorological onslaughts.

An often disregarded but highly valued condition of trees is their ability to host other life forms. The encino texmole

is home to fungi massing in its roots, lichens and mosses sheltering in its thick bark (fig. 3), climbing lianas and epiphytes perching on its twisting branches, and ferns, sedums, orchids, and bromeliads encrusting its trunk and stout branches. The abundant litter of its fallen leaves forms nutritious soil that nourishes other plants. Insects, reptiles, and amphibians inhabit the tree (fig. 4). Birds nest and perch on the branches. Small mammals climb it and build their dens in the rocks where it stands. It is an "organism habitat," or, as Abel Rodríguez reminds us in the preface to this book, a "tree of life and abundance."

Groves of encino texmole, with their deciduous branches and leaves, supply sacred shade with shifting patterns of light and shade across the rocky terrain where they thrive. These species supply environmental services: collecting, filtering, and transporting water to the subsoil—a key and noble capability in their resistance and adaptability to the environment. They require little to no irrigation and are a critical habitat keystone species that makes a significant contribution to the urban dynamics of the Mexico City metropolis.

The resilience, environmental services, and aesthetic values of encino texmole must be considered by landscape architects in the future. For now, I am protecting them when I find them in the Pedregal, and we are propagating the species at our university nurseries in an attempt to make it available for projects (fig. 5). Perhaps over the next several decades, our work will cultivate a wider use of the tree, as others have done for species such as *Gleditsia triacanthos* in the United States and other species around the world.

The recognition of oaks as trees that supply great value to the design of landscapes is gaining traction in Mexico. It is crucial to find the most suitable local species, given the vast diversity of the genus, that can be grown in sufficient quantities for each region of Mexico. These magnificent organisms—capable of living for centuries—will witness the evolution of human consciousness and serve as a reminder of our interconnectedness with the natural world.

Romero Rangel, S., E. C. Rojas Zenteno, and L. E. Rubio Licona. 2015. "Encinos de México." Mexico City: Universidad Nacional Autónoma de México.

5

Robinia pseudoacacia

black locust

Traveling Species: Native and Invasive Actors in the Landscape

Antonio Longo / Milan, Italy

190

Antonio Longo is a professor in the Department of Architecture and Urban Studies at the Politecnico de Milano and coordinator of the Laurea Magistrale Programme in Landscape Architecture and Landscape Heritage at the Scuola di Architettura Urbanistica Ingegneria delle Costruzioni.

The black locust is a plant of great adaptability and beauty. Its bark is rough, its trunk is twisted or linear, and its young branches are thorny (fig. 1). It has an extraordinary ability to spread, both through seeds and suckers. It tolerates dry soils,

1

breaks, and cuts. It attracts bees with its fragrant flowers, and the honey produced from those flowers is highly valued. The wood is hard and the biomass is good for burning. The black locust is a leguminous plant: its roots, in symbiosis with bacteria, fix nitrogen and enrich the soil. Because it does not like shade and does not have a long life, it is repeatedly replaced, thus promoting the formation of complex forest environments.

The tree is endemic to the Appalachian Mountains of North America and was brought to Europe in the seventeenth century, where it has since spread. In 1601, Jean Robin (1550–1629), herbalist and botanist to French royalty, obtained the first specimens (from seeds brought from New France). One of those specimens still exists in Paris—at Square René-Viviani—and is considered the oldest living tree in the city. Black locust was later introduced to Italy at the Botanical Garden of Padua in 1662. Linnaeus's genus name is dedicated to its French discoverer, while the species name refers to its similarity to the acacia. After its introduction to Europe, it accompanied the evolution of landscape architecture—flanking military technology, hydraulics, engineering, and civil architecture. Later, it was used in the consolidation of canals and in the creation

2

of living piles. From the mid-nineteenth century onwards, railroad embankments and escarpments in Europe were stabilized by robust plantings of locust. Thus it became a traveling companion to the expansion of railroads and highways. Even Alwin Seifert, the landscape architect of the Third Reich's highways, recommended in 1934 (despite his mania for native plants) that it be used for embankments with unstable soils.

In Europe it has long been a stigmatized plant, and its tendency to grow and colonize abandoned pastures and uncultivated areas led to its identification as alien and invasive. However, more recent ecological and forestry studies have reevaluated the problem by emphasizing the qualities that make this plant the true protagonist of the "third landscape" and the regeneration of degraded urban environments: as early as the 1990s, Gilles Clément was using the locust's mobility and capacity for colonization in his Parisian park projects.

In the mid-1990s, at the beginning of my work between urban planning and landscape, I studied and designed the restoration of the park at Villa Contarini in Piazzola sul Brenta, on the Veneto plain (fig. 2). It is a palimpsest of works, beginning in the late sixteenth century with an early

3

4

Palladian building owned by the Contarini family and then transformed in the late nineteenth century by the industrial city under the direction of Paolo Camerini (1868–1937), a wealthy industrialist and politician who was the promoter of the city's modernization.

The park occupies 100 ha of the ancient bed of the Brenta River and is structured by two axes: the north-south perspective—central, symmetrical, and parallel to the course of the river—which marks the villa's geometry within the surrounding territory, and the east-west axis, which defines the boundaries between garden and countryside (fig. 3). The latter axis is a nineteenth-century invention, designed by the owner with the support of agricultural engineers and local nurseries. It consists of 1,000 m of meadow path flanked by a canal and shaded by a double row of *Robinia pseudoacacia* var. *umbraculifera* (fig. 4). Alternating on the two sides of the path, the planting is 5 m wide, and the plants have, over time, been steadily pruned. Planted between 1880 and 1890, the row was already at the end of its life cycle twenty-five years ago and would have had to be entirely replaced for an authentic restoration. However, the many individuals responsible for management and projects since then have made other choices. These plants, formed by time, hollowed and damaged by cutting, covered by ivy and wisteria, inhabited by woodpeckers and insects, have survived, replaced when necessary by new plantings in acceptance of the unevenness of natural succession (fig. 5). Since then, these nearly 150-year-old trees have bloomed and leafed out powerfully, marking the edges of the park and the geographical distance between the villa and the mountain horizon. The locust trees in Villa Contarini's park are still there, silent and eloquent, witnesses of the twentieth century, nourishing the soil, enriching the ecosystem, measuring time and space, as actors in the landscape (fig. 6).

5

6

Samanea saman

rain tree, umbrella tree, monkeypod, saman

The Giant Umbrella of the Tropics

Fa Likitswat / Bangkok, Thailand

Fa Likitswat is an assistant professor of landscape architecture in the Thammasat Design School's Faculty of Architecture and Planning at Thammasat University in Thailand.

1 

A rain tree at my grandparent's stupas grew from a small tree to a large tree during my childhood. Grown from a seed spread by birds, the tree now crowns and shades the stupas that sit atop a mound and beside a pond with vistas of the mountain (fig. 1). There are now groves of rain trees spreading through our family farm. My parents selected and grew large trees that welcomed birds to the farm, and rain trees became a sign of peace and freedom for our family's beliefs.

The rain tree has one of the largest ratios of canopy diameter to height of any tree. Mature trees can reach a canopy diameter of 80 m and a height of 25–30 m, or an approximately three-to-one ratio of diameter to height. There are giant specimens across the subtropics and tropics. The underside of the canopy of open-grown rain trees has a remarkable horizontality that parallels the ground, with a gently sloping, parasol-shaped crown above. Since rain trees can also grow in swampy, hydric, acid soil, the tree can grow as a riparian corridor tree with a broad, shallow root system (fig. 2).

The undersides of the leaves have a soft, velvety texture The fine leaflets decay rapidly—a characteristic that can be beneficial for urban drainage systems, since the leaves will not clog drainage channels, which endears them to municipal agencies. A remarkable characteristic of the leaves is that the leaflets are light-sensitive; they close on cloudy days, allowing rain to fall through the canopy to the ground below—one of the possible derivations of the common name "rain tree" (fig. 3).

2 

3

In addition to this light sensitivity, two other characteristics of the rain tree are its fluffy bright pink and white flowers, which festoon the branches when in bloom like thousands of tail feathers or feather dusters, and the sweet edible fruit, which grows in large, thick, leathery seedpods that resemble giant pea pods.

The rain tree is not native to Southeast Asia, but it is common to see its spreading canopy shading streets and canals in Thailand, Malaysia, and Singapore. The experience of a rain tree tunnel along the road is a memorable everyday event when traveling through the southern corridor of Thailand. The shade from their dense canopies creates a cool microclimate in tropical urban areas.

In Bangkok, the iconic hundred-year-old rain trees on Wireless Road face unhealthy conditions in the face of city development, road expansion, compacted soil, and poor pruning. The trees in the middle of the road are suffering while nearby, on the grounds of embassies and other properties, well-maintained mature trees with more space for their shallow roots achieve full size with good health. To extend the rain tree corridor on Wireless Road, I designed 25 cm-caliper rain trees that were transplanted as new street trees for a hotel project opposite the former British Embassy (fig. 4). The planting distance for rain trees to grow into an upright form can be from 8 to 10 m. Rich and airy planting soil was carefully designed to accommodate the new root system.

For a health and wellness project alongside Thailand's Bang Pakong River, I used the rain tree in several ways: along a riparian corridor, to define a boundary, to mark the entrance, and to shade parking and outdoor seating by the river (fig. 5). Across 10.88 ha, two sizes of *Samanea saman* were selected. Trees measuring 10–15 cm in caliper and 6 m in height were planted along the street and to shade parking. Larger trees measuring

4

5

25–30 cm in caliper and 8 m in height anchored the entrance and provided shade along the river. The spacing of the trees was varied between 30 and 50 m to give more room for growth. These rain trees were augmented with other species to diversify the plant community, which had previously been a monoculture of coconut orchards.

The rain tree was introduced to Southeast Asia over a hundred years ago and has proven to be a productive and valuable tree for both farmlands and cities. Its extensive canopy enhances the well-being of humans and urban wildlife; it is a tree favored by herons and other large birds, for instance. My childhood experience of monitoring the growth of rain trees on my family farm reminds me of the contributions it can make in a vibrant, green city. We can imagine birds nesting and thriving in the same green canopy whose shade shelters our urban landscapes.

Schinus molle

Peruvian peppertree, aguaribay

A Maker of Atmospheres

Mónica Bertolino /
Buenos Aires, Argentina

Mónica Bertolino is a professor of architectural, urban and landscape projects at the National University of Córdoba, and in the master's program at the National University of the Littoral in Argentina. She is a founding partner of Bertolino-Barrado.

1 

This tree, native to the central region of South America, is called aguaribay in Argentina, where it grows wild from the province of Córdoba (in the center of the country) to the province of Jujuy (in the north). Of all the names it has acquired in the other countries and regions where it is also native, I like "aguaribay," a melodious name with indigenous reminiscences of Guarani and Quechua.

For centuries it was highly appreciated by pre-Hispanic South American cultures due to its multiple medicinal and culinary properties, and also as a source of natural dyes and essential oils. It also marks the presence of nearby aquifers and other water sources, since its deep roots are able to take the moisture it seeks from deep underground. It can grow in sandy and dry soils, which it also helps to sustain and ameliorate.

The architecture of the tree is very attractive in its form, spatiality, texture, and color (fig. 1). These qualities combine with the beneficial properties recognized by our ancestors. But the sensory character created by its attributes and behavior is what I consider its greater contribution and what attracts me the most. It has a relaxed silhouette and a weeping shape that can reach between 8 and 10 m in height, with a generous canopy of similar width. Its sinuous and sometimes formless or winding trunk is covered by a scaly bark that releases a very fragrant resin when peeled off.

The hanging branches resemble those of the willow, and the foliage has light green compound leaves attached to very delicate pendulous twigs. It blossoms in the spring with clusters of small yellowish flowers that later form aromatic fruits with a sweet and spicy flavor, pink peppers suitable for culinary use, to which it owes another of its names, "Peruvian peppertree." It has great tolerance to drought. It reproduces naturally through the dispersion of seeds by birds (ornithochory). Its medicinal properties are still valued today.

Its ornamental use is widespread but its distinctive contribution is its appeal to all the senses: sight, touch, smell, taste, hearing. Its structure and spatiality, together with its movement and fragrances, create a singular atmosphere.

I appreciate its generous figure, with its semitransparent textured canopy, like a mane without sharp edges that sways sensitively in the breeze, generating a fresh music of soft rain. I like to see it move its pendulous branches and listen to the sonority of its foliage. I like to caress

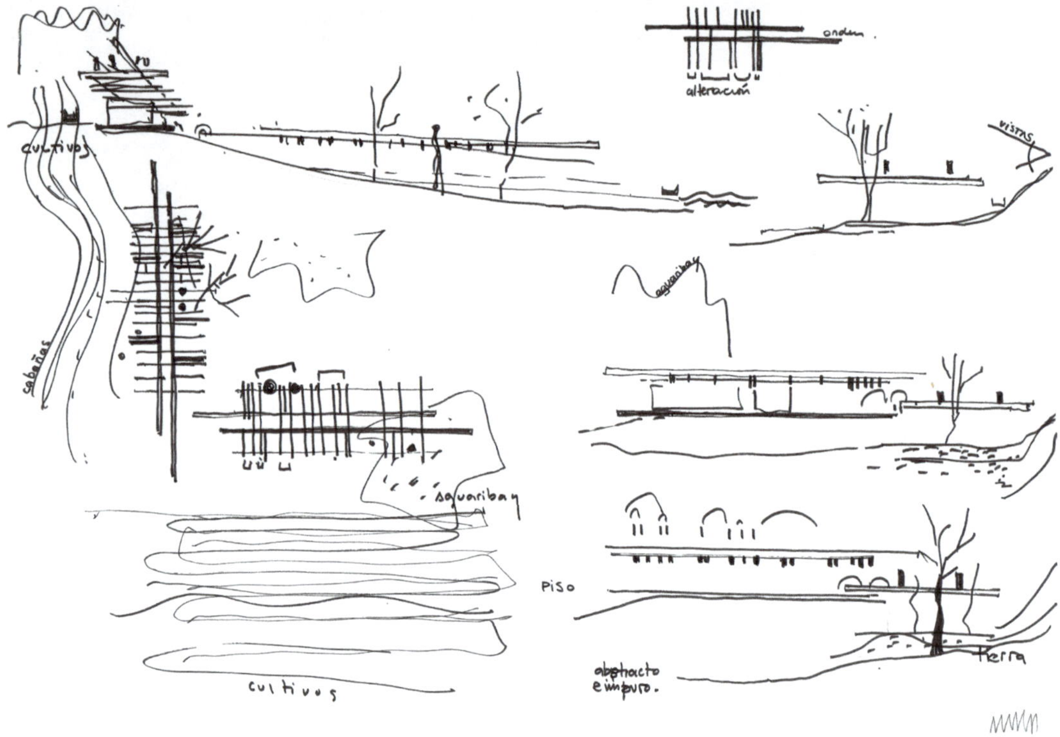

3

its leaves and fruit and to be left with the unmistakable aroma of its resin on my hands.

Although its use has spread to other temperate climates and it adorns the streets and parks of other regions, its presence refers to the geographical and cultural contexts of its origin. For me personally, it is closely linked to the experiences of my own region in Córdoba, from the mountains or sierras to the city. This undoubtedly also influences my preferences.

In our proposals, every time we choose the aguaribay, we are thinking about the multiple qualities it contributes, the atmosphere it creates, and the multisensory perception it provokes, which accentuates the living experience of each place.

We have included it in projects for parks and public spaces in the city and in
the mountains. Its mere presence gener- 2
ates a special atmosphere that reinforces the experience of the place. For the area around Puente Sarmiento, a bridge that marks one of the entrances to the center of the city of Córdoba, we proposed a forest of aguaribays on the banks of the Suquía River, leaving a circular clearing as a square at the head of the bridge.

In our project for an educational farm in Capilla del Monte, in the Córdoban mountains, we began by interpreting the place with the aim of working in dialogue with nature (figs. 2 and 3). The presence of an existing aguaribay on the site, together with other native trees such as chañar (*Geoffroea decorticans*), quebracho (*Schinopsis* sp.), and algarrobo (*Prosopis* sp.), gave us a set of guidelines, allowing us to trace the proposal to the point where an abstract concrete structure gives way to the trees that crisscross it, creating a counterpoint with the roughness of the trunks or their unique foliage. In this particular case, we celebrate the presence of the aguaribay that presides over one of the complex's two pavilions and exalts the sensory character to which the proposal aspires (figs. 4 and 5).

Aguaribay, a generous tree that surrounds you with its sensual and fragrant foliage: prodigal in properties, a maker of atmospheres.

4

5

Theobroma cacao

cacao

The Tree of the Golden Seed

Ernesto Bilbao / Quito, Ecuador

Ernesto Bilbao is an assistant professor of architecture at Auburn University's School of Architecture, Planning, and Landscape Architecture, and founding principal of Estudio Ernesto Bilbao.

In 2012, Ecuador's Coordinating Ministry of Heritage appointed my studio to design the Jardín del Cacao y Chocolate (Garden of cacao and chocolate). This project was conceived to display and promote ancestral traditions relating to the cultivation of a highly flavorful variety of cacao called *fino de aroma* on small parcels called *chacras* (also known as swidden or home gardens) by indigenous Quechua communities and their neighbors in Ecuadorian Amazonia. The design entailed modifying a municipal *chacra* in Arosemena Tola, a canton in the province of Napo, where cacao trees cohabited in perfect balance within a small 4.86 ha parcel of rainforest. The project asked a challenging question: How to design a landscape in an existing landscape?

The design of the Jardín del Cacao y Chocolate required research on the crucial role of cacao trees in thousand-year-old cultural landscapes that harmoniously integrate agricultural production with the Amazon rainforest (figs. 1 and 2). Here, indigenous peoples adapted and managed the rainforest to sustain resources, such as soil, and plants, such as cacao, without affecting its original biodiversity. *Chacras* refute the common assumption that Amazonia is a purely natural landscape, demonstrating instead that it is the result of human agency. The artisanal cultivation and production of flavorful cacao within these ancestral landscapes differs from the techniques of Western monoculture and is an important instrument of household food security and cultural identification for local and indigenous communities.

The cultivation of cacao *fino de aroma*, combined with other productive species within *chacras*, has positioned Ecuador as one of the world's most important producers of this type of caca. Ecuador's history has always been connected with cacao trees and their *pepas de oro*, or golden seeds (fig. 3). This relationship began when the production of "creole" or ordinary cacao led to a cacao boom, consolidating Ecuador as the world's largest exporter of the fruit between the 1890s and 1920s. Ecuador's *fino de aroma* trees and seeds

1

2

have once again put the country back on the international chocolate map.

Recent archaeological studies of residue in pottery suggest that humans were harvesting, consuming, and trading cacao in Ecuador's Amazon rainforest as much as five thousand years ago. From there, cacao and its seeds spread as an exotic product to Mesoamerica, where the Mayans and Aztecs used it as currency and as a sacred drink. The West's appreciation of chocolate began when the Spanish conquistadors tasted *xocolatl*, the spicy Aztec chocolate drink, and introduced it to Europe in the sixteenth century. Consequently, as Irene Caselli posits (2013), Ecuadorian Amazonia played a significant historical "role in introducing chocolate to the West."

Currently, cacao trees and their cultivation support approximately a hundred thousand small farmers and other participants in the supply chain (fig. 4). Because of its superior taste, cacao *fino de aroma* has helped unusual entrepreneurs from Quechua communities produce valuable gourmet chocolate such as Kallari and Paccari. Much like wine, "chocolate reflects the flavors of the landscapes where cacao seeds are grown, dried, and fermented—they can taste 'like fruits' or have a 'nutty flavor'" (Caselli 2013).

Cacao trees in thousand-year-old *chacras* grow to a height of 6–12 m, with irregular branching and an open, asymmetrical canopy. Two main features characterize the cacao. First, its oblong, leathery leaves can measure up to 30 cm in length and are a dramatic red when young. Second, its fruits are in the form of elongated pods, or *cherelles*, that range in color from bright yellow to deep purple as they grow up to 35 cm, ripening in less than six months. These pods grow tightly stacked against the trunk, almost like ornamental parasitic necklaces. Each pod holds twenty to sixty edible seeds, from which the cacao tree gets the name *Theobroma*, "the food of the gods." After cultivating, fermenting, and drying these seeds, or cocoa beans, Quechua farmers use them to produce cocoa powder, cocoa butter, and chocolate.

3

The response to the design of the Jardín del Cacao y Chocolate thus seemed obvious. It relies on a pathway through various pavilions that choreographs movement through the productive forest, which visualizes the process of cacao cultivation and its transformation into artisanal chocolate (fig. 5). This path allows the visitor to have a more intimate experience with the cacao trees and recognize the larger natural, historical, and cultural beauty of the landscape of the *chacra* and Ecuador's Amazonian rainforest.

Caselli, I. 2013. "Is Ecuador Home to the World's Best Chocolate?" BBC News, June 6, 2013. https://www.bbc.com/news/world-latin-america-22733002.

4

5

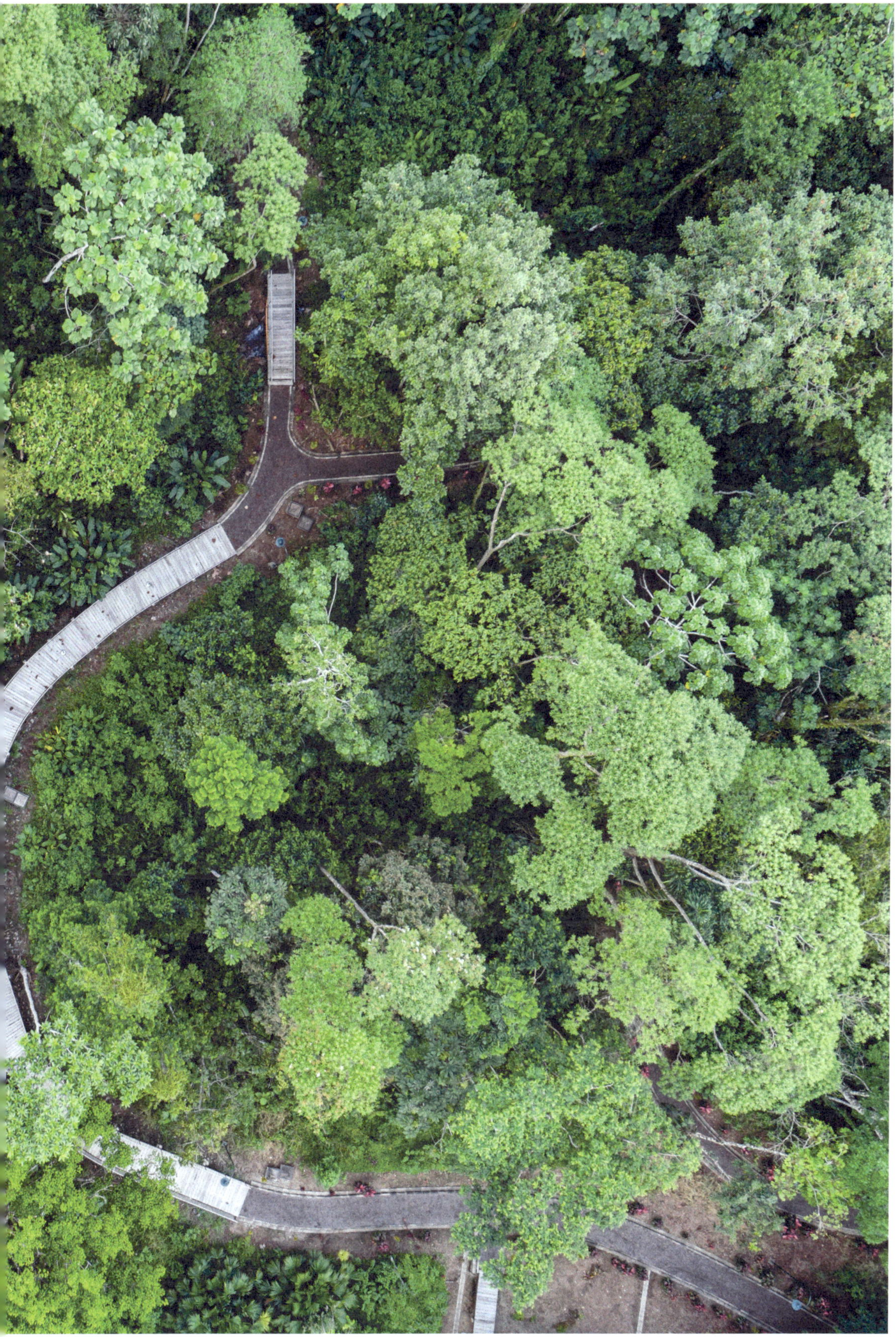

Tipuana tipu

tipuana, tipa

An Ideal Companion for the Cities of Tomorrow

Mounia Bennani / Rabat, Morocco

Mounia Bennani is a landscape architect with a doctorate in geography from the École nationale supérieure du paysage in Versailles. She is a founding principal of MBpaysage and member of the Association of Landscape Architects of Morocco.

Tipuana tipu looks like the black locust (*Robinia pseudoacacia*) but has no thorns. Originally from South America, it is now found in southern Europe and on the other side of the Mediterranean, in Morocco. It is resilient and likes all types of soils, even salty ones. It tolerates both humidity and drought, as well as significant temperature variations ranging from frost in winter to over forty degrees in summer. In summer, when it covers itself with its thousand and one small yellow-orange flowers, it

1

enhances our streets and gardens and attracts pollinating insects. In winter, without its foliage, it draws a dark and textured silhouette. Its graphic habit reveals a cracked grayish trunk and slightly drooping cut branches (fig. 1). Its leaves, made up of leaflets, have a soft green color that lets the sun shine through and illuminate the foliage. Its powerful roots make it an ideal tree for holding the soil in place.

The tipuana was introduced to Morocco with the creation of European-style cities under the French Protectorate (1912–56). Outside the medinas, a new model of garden city was born with the French landscape architect Jean-Claude Nicolas Forestier (1861–1930), who, in 1913, experimented with a concept for a "system of parks," in reference to the American park system that Frederick Law Olmsted (1822–1903) helped to create. A continuous network of planted avenues, public parks, and wooded areas was to form the landscape fabric of the modern city. To shade the roads and emphasize the perspectives, the French planted evergreens (*Ficus benjamina* and *Schinus terebinthifolia*), palms (*Phoenix canariensis* and *Washingtonia filifera*), and flowering trees such as *Jacaranda mimosifolia*, remarkable for its blue-violet blooms.

It was in Rabat, Morocco's capital, that I discovered *Tipuana tipu* for the first time, in the Hay Ryad district, which was built in the 1980s. The tipuanas there were planted in an unusual staggered pattern. I was amazed by their spreading parasol-shaped habit, their light foliage, and, above all, their spectacular yellow flowers in June (fig. 2).

2

Back from my studies in France and working on projects for my agency, I first tested *Tipuana tipu* in southern Morocco as part of the creation of a new green city, Mine Verte, in Khouribga. The challenge was to find trees able to adapt to the hot and semiarid climate and the poor and stony soils. I used rows of tipuanas to

3

4

5

structure the avenues of future districts. Planted ten years ago, today the tipuanas form beautiful, shady, cool garden avenues, pleasant to see and live in (fig. 3).

My most recent tipuana plantings are at Ghabat Chabab Park in Marrakesh. It is an old olive grove of 120 ha planted the day after independence, which we redesigned as an urban park. I used *Tipuana tipu* as a horticultural tree in isolation, in rows to accentuate perspectival views of the Atlas mountains, and also in more forestlike plantings, mixed with species endemic to Morocco (including *Ceratonia siliqua*, *Argania spinosa*, and *Vachellia gummifera*). Its rapid growth has created a high stratum that protects the smaller species. I am delighted to see the effect created by young tipuana trees in a square, barely three years after they were planted. The young trees, whose trunks measured 14 cm in diameter when planted, have doubled in size. They provide beautiful foliage and valuable shade for visitors (fig. 4).

My most moving experience remains my meeting, in Marrakesh, with one of Morocco's oldest tipuanas. About ten years ago, on the famous square Jemaa el-Fnaa, my gaze was drawn to an impressive silhouette with light foliage soaring towards the sky. I moved closer: it was a *Tipuana tipu*, probably planted under the French Protectorate in the 1920s (fig. 5). At a height of 21 m, it looms over the *Phoenix canariensis* and *Ficus nitida* planted around it at the same period. Its trunk measures 8.2 m in diameter, and its crown spreads out over an area of 28 m^2, with a resilience and a majesty that command respect and humility. This living monument has managed to withstand time and the vicissitudes of the climate. Over the years, it has created around it a pleasant and peaceful environment. By its presence, its shade, and its freshness, which I expressed in drawings, it protects living beings, human and nonhuman, who have lived alongside it for several generations. This invaluable living heritage for the city of Marrakesh is, to my surprise, unknown to the inhabitants.

In the context of global warming, *Tipuana tipu* becomes a universal tree, an ideal companion to help our cities of tomorrow live better.

"Loving trees," writes Francis Hallé (2011, back cover), "is another way of loving man."*

Hallé, F. 2011. *Du bon usage des arbres. Un plaidoyer à l'attention des élus et des énarques*. Arles: Actes Sud.

* "Aimer les arbres, c'est une autre façon d'aimer l'homme."

Triadica sebifera

Chinese tallow

Tree of Poetry and Painting

Yifeng Lin / Shanghai, China

Yifeng Lin is a landscape architect, founding principal of YIYU design studio, and honorary adjunct assistant professor at Hong Kong University.

1

If a tree can be described as a friend, then the Chinese tallow is the kind of friend that reveals more charms the longer you know it. Its unpretentious beauty and consistent performance make it a steadfast and reliable selection for landscapes.

The Chinese tallow originates in East Asia and is portrayed in Chinese poetry and ink paintings. It is popular in romantic scenes due to its year-round beauty and picturesque habit. It is also an inspiring tree that provides multiple sensory experiences: you can hear its rattling leaves on a breezy day in the spring; you can feel a range of coolness under its airy canopy in the summer, and you can see its unusual color explosion of green, orange, and red foliage in the autumn. Its beautiful character and romantic qualities make the Chinese tallow a tree that sensitizes us to nature and to poetic imaginations of time:

月落烏啼霜滿天， At moonset cry the crows,
streaking the frosty sky.

江楓漁火對愁眠。 Dimly lit fishing boats
'neath tallows sadly lie.

姑蘇城外寒山寺， Beyond the city walls,
from Temple of Cold Hill.

夜半鐘聲到客船。 Bells break the ship-borne
roamer's dream and midnight still.

(Adapted from Zhang 2005)*

Though the tallow has so many distinctive qualities, it blends humbly in nature. Its structure consists of strong sculptural trunks. Its twigs are so fine that the canopy becomes almost transparent and merges into the background in winter and early spring. This characteristic transparency continues with the emergence of thin, delicate leaves that lend airiness

2

* In this classic poem by Zhang Ji (fl. 715–79), the word 楓 (*fēng*) has traditionally been translated into English as "maple." However, in ancient Chinese poetry, 楓 can refer generally to trees with red leaves in autumn, rather than to any particular species. Considering that the trees in this poem are growing along the riverbank, it seems quite likely that Zhang actually had Chinese tallows in mind.

to the canopy and give rise to wonderful layerings of arboreal space. Like watercolors, the tree overlaps with other trees and creates fantastic depth of light, shade, and muted colors in parks and gardens.

This transparent blending quality also appears in autumn, when the tallow's leaves gradually change their color from bright green to sugary orange to scarlet and dark purple. As the color gradient changes across the season, the tree becomes a barometer for the smooth transition from summer to autumn. This special quality also gives Chinese tallow a wonderful ability to mediate the chromatic blending of trees with different fall colors in parks or gardens. For instance, when planted between stands of red maple and

ginkgo, the multicolored tallow bridges the pure red of the maples and the golden yellow of the ginkgos.

Chinese tallow is also satisfying to scrutinize more closely. Its distinctive diamond-shaped leaves make it beautiful and identifiable. Because the leaves are so light and fine, they catch the slightest wind—like green feathers hanging on the tree—and create lovely movements with a joyful rustling on breezy days. The fluttering leaves allow sunlight to penetrate the canopy and provide dappled light and shade under the tree. This airy quality makes tallow an excellent selection to create cool areas for sitting in the summer.

At Shanghai MOMA Museum Waterfront Park, YIYU used tallow as the featured trees in a central water garden, where they are planted in a grid to embrace the reflection pond in the center, creating a soft ring of green that strengthens and frames the pond and the sky (figs. 1 and 2). The leafy canopy shapes a quiet and tranquil interior space. When you walk through the trees to the water, like entering a sanctuary protected by nature, the perfectly strong yet gentle wall of tallows creates a structure that is both spiritual and poetic.

We also chose to use tallow in this project because of the vivid mixture of autumn colors that follows its bright green summer canopy (fig. 3). Like a gigantic mirror, the pond reflects the beautiful autumn colors of the trees. As leaves start to fall, they float on the water and overlap with the reflection. The juxtaposition between the reflected and the floating creates dreamy yet vibrant color combinations on the water: red-orange reflections from the canopy and purple and scarlet from the fallen leaves.

Snow-like seeds hang on the branches through the winter, after the leaves have fallen, and will remain until spring. These seeds provide an unusual mist-like effect in the landscape. They provide food for birds, although they are toxic to humans. This winter effect, rare for a deciduous tree, and usefulness as a food resource for avian species make Chinese tallow an exceptional tree in winter.

Zhang Ji's poem depicts the fisherman's boats lying sadly beneath the trees at midnight. This captures the mood of being under these trees. As in many landscapes, one of the most potent spatial situations is the space between the ground and the canopy of trees. With these qualities—perfect seasonal effects, sensational shapes, textural details, and sustenance for wildlife, the Chinese tallow rewards those lingering beneath it with painterly poetics.

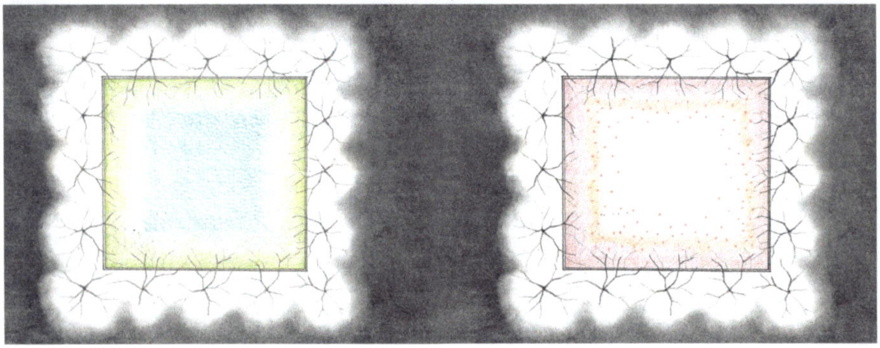

3

Left: summer; right: autumn.

Zhang J. 2005. "Mooring by Maple Bridge at Night," translated by Xu Yuanchong. In *Diǎnjí yīng yì yánjiū / Studies on Translation of Chinese Classics into English*, edited by Wang Rongpei and Li Zhengshuan, 1:164. Hebei: Hebei University Press.

Tree Index

Hans Friedl / Chicago USA

Acer macrophyllum (bigleaf maple)

Family:
Sapindaceae

Native range:
Coastal Pacific Northwest of North America

Bigleaf maples grow to 15–25 m tall and are the largest maples indigenous to North America. They are rarely found more than a few hundred kilometers east of the Pacific Ocean. Their leaves are the largest of all North American maples, emerging in burgundy, flushing out to vibrant bright green, maturing to deep green, and turning yellow-orange in the fall.

Seasonal foliage color
Spring | Summer | Fall | Winter

Aesculus hippocastanum (horse chestnut)

Family:
Sapindaceae

Native range:
Balkans in Europe

The horse chestnut's oval crown can grow up to 22 m tall. The showy white flowers extend in upright terminal panicles in mid-spring atop branches sporting palmate compound leaves with oblong and ovate leaflets. The fruits ripen throughout the year in globular dehiscent capsules covered with sharp spines.

Seasonal foliage color
Spring | Summer | Fall | Winter

Betula pendula (European white birch)

Family: Betulaceae

Native range: Europe and Asia

Growing up to 10 m tall, the European white birch thrives in wetter areas. The exfoliating white bark peels away in papery strips, and mature trees display a blackish-gray furrowing of the bark near the base of the tree. Ovate, glabrous, toothed green leaves hang at the ends of pendulous branches.

Seasonal foliage color
Spring | Summer | Fall | Winter

Bursera simaruba (gumbo-limbo, copal, papelillo rojo, palo mulato)

Family:
Burseraceae

Native range:
Neotropics

This fast-growing species can grow up to 30 m tall and has shiny, exfoliating red bark. Leaves are spirally arranged and pinnate with seven to eleven leaflets, which are broad and ovate. Shallow and dense root systems make copal wind-tolerant, an important characteristic in hurricane-prone regions.

Seasonal foliage color
Spring | Summer | Fall | Winter

Ceiba pentandra (kapok, ceiba)

Family:
Malvaceae

Native range:
Central America and northern South America

The kapok tree can grow to a staggering 38 m tall, in rare cases reaching as high as 70 m. Large buttresses at the base of the tree support spiny pale gray trunks. Creamy white bell-shaped flowers bloom before palmate compound leaves appear.

Seasonal foliage color
Spring | Summer | Fall | Winter

Cercidiphyllum japonicum (katsura)

Family:
Cercidiphyllaceae

Native range:
Japan, Korea, and China

The katsura is an understory tree, often with clusters of trunks, that can grow to 16 m tall. Its cordate, round-oval leaves emerge reddish purple in spring, mature to medium green with a bluish tinge in summer, and transition to shades of gold, orange, and red in fall.

Seasonal foliage color

Spring Summer Fall Winter

Cupressus sempervirens (Mediterranean cypress)

Family:
Cupressaceae

Native range:
Southern Europe and western Asia

The Mediterranean cypress is a fastigiate evergreen conifer that can grow 20 m tall. Foliage clumps in thick masses, dark green in color, and scale-like leaves emerge on rounded shoots.

Seasonal foliage color

Spring Summer Fall Winter

Cyrtophyllum fragrans (tembusu, ironwood)

Family:
Gentianaceae

Native range:
Southeast Asia

The tembusu can grow to 25 m tall, with a distinctive branching pattern in which limbs grow outwards and then upwards like fingers. This slow-growing tree lives in the lowlands, and the bark of the trunk is deeply fissured with vertical ridges. Its green and bluish-hued leaves are arranged in whorls.

Seasonal foliage color

Spring Summer Fall Winter

Ficus carica (common fig)

Family: Moraceae

Native range: Mediterranean and southwest Asia

Fig trees can grow between 7 and 10 m tall. Their smooth white bark and dark green, deeply lobed leaves have created shade for humans and animals for centuries. The desirable tear-shaped fruit grows with a green skin that may ripen to a dark purple or brown and is associated with many myths and legends.

Seasonal foliage color

Spring Summer Fall Winter

Ficus macrophylla (Moreton Bay fig)

Family:
Moraceae

Native range:
Eastern Australia

The Moreton Bay fig often germinates in the canopy of another tree before connecting with the ground and growing to more than 60 m tall. Its buttress roots help support the enormous biomass above, but it also drops aerial roots that thicken into supplementary trunks.

Seasonal foliage color

Spring Summer Fall Winter

Gleditsia triacanthos (honey locust)

Family:
Fabaceae

Native range:
Central and eastern
North America

Honey locusts grow to 20–25 m tall with an open, spreading crown of pinnate and bipinnate leaves that turn bright yellow early in the fall. The species has sharp thorns and leathery seedpods, although thornless and podless varieties are more common in contemporary landscapes.

Seasonal foliage color
Spring Summer Fall Winter

Handroanthus serratifolius (curarire, ipê, poui, pau d'arco)

Family:
Bignoniaceae

Native range:
Central and South America

As one of the largest and strongest tropical trees, the curarire can grow upwards of 46 m tall. The blooms erupt in a storm of yellow every spring, marking the change of the seasons. The finely serrated leaves give this tree its species name.

Seasonal foliage color
Spring Summer Fall Winter

Liquidambar styraciflua (sweetgum)

Family:
Altingiaceae

Native range:
Eastern United States
and Mexico

Sweetgums can grow to 18–22 m tall in moist and shaded low woodlands. The star-shaped foliage turns dark green in the summer before transitioning to a brilliant mix of yellows, oranges, purples, and reds in the fall. Flowers are replaced by hard, spiny, spherical fruits that can persist throughout winter.

Seasonal foliage color
Spring Summer Fall Winter

Mauritia flexuosa (buriti, moriche palm, ité palm, miriti)

Family:
Arecaceae

Native range:
Tropical South America

The buriti is a slow-growing dioecious palm tree that can be found in wet areas, where it grows to 35 m high. The large leaves are used to make thatch, ropes, hammocks, belts, hats, baskets, and other useful items, while the straight-grained wood can be used as construction material.

Seasonal foliage color
Spring Summer Fall Winter

Pinus pinea (stone pine)

Family:
Pinaceae

Native range:
Mediterranean
and southern Europe

This coniferous evergreen can exceed 25 m in height as it pushes its umbrella canopy into the air. The bushy globe of the young tree's foliage turns into a broad, flat canopy in maturity, held up by a stout red-brown trunk. The edible nuts of the stone pine have been harvested for centuries.

Seasonal foliage color
Spring Summer Fall Winter

Pinus thunbergii (Japanese black pine, matsu-zukuri)

Family:
Pinaceae

Native range:
Coastal Japan and Korea

The Japanese black pine can grow to be one of the most staggering overstory trees in its natural range, reaching heights of 40 m. Its bending and asymmetrical trunk forms elegant lines as the tree ascends with a spreading canopy and pendulous branches.

Seasonal foliage color
Spring Summer Fall Winter

Platanus ×acerifolia (London planetree)

Family:
Platanaceae

Naturalized range:
Widely distributed across temperate and subtropical regions globally

The London planetree can grow to 22–30 m tall, with a stout trunk supporting a rounded habit. Plates of outer bark exfoliate to reveal the mottled white bark below, which contributes to its success as an urban tree found around the world.

Seasonal foliage color
Spring Summer Fall Winter

Plinia cauliflora (jabuticabeira)

Family:
Myrtaceae

Native range:
Brazil and Bolivia

Jabuticabeira are subtropical evergreens that tend to grow in dense, bushy, and rounded forms 3–7 m tall. Because it is a cauliflorous species, its globose purple fruits grow directly from the trunk and larger branches.

Seasonal foliage color
Spring Summer Fall Winter

Populus alba (white poplar, silver poplar, sepidar)

Family:
Salicaceae

Native range:
Northern Africa and central Asia

The smooth green-white or gray-white trunks of the silver poplar can reach heights of 15–30 m. Their smooth bark is interrupted by a pattern of diamond-shaped marks that become blackish and fissured with age. The tree spreads through root suckers to form clonal colonies.

Seasonal foliage color
Spring Summer Fall Winter

Populus deltoides (eastern cottonwood)

Family: Salicaceae

Native range:
Eastern, central, and southwestern United States

The triangular leaves of the eastern cottonwood can be seen fluttering high in the air, between 22 and 30 m up. Large cracked and fissured trunks quickly emerge in the most inhospitable environments making this one of the first species to renaturalize landscapes. Found most often in bottomlands, the cottonwood can endure a range of environmental conditions.

Seasonal foliage color
Spring Summer Fall Winter

Populus nigra var. *italica* (Lombardy poplar)

Family:
Salicaceae

Native range:
Europe and central Asia

Lombardy poplars can grow to be 20–30 m tall in boggy lowland areas, forest margins, fields, or roadsides throughout Europe and western Asia. The bark on mature trees can become dark gray, knotted, deeply fissured, gnarled, and burred, which contrasts with its bright-yellow foliage in the autumn.

Seasonal foliage color
Spring Summer Fall Winter

Psidium friedrichsthalianum (Costa Rican guava, cas)

Family:
Myrtaceae

Native range:
Costa Rica

The cas grows to be 6–12 m tall and is found primarily in Costa Rica but also in surrounding countries in Central America. The round fruit is commonly used to make a sour and refreshing drink.

Seasonal foliage color
Spring Summer Fall Winter

Quercus agrifolia (coast live oak, yuukiš, yuukš, bellota de encino)

Family:
Fagaceae

Native range:
Coastal southwestern California

Coast live oak are long-lived trees found between the Sierra Nevada mountain range and the Pacific Ocean in southern California. Mature trees can grow to be 10–25 m tall, with contorted and gnarled trunks and branches. They frequently inhabit the coastal hills and plains, where coastal fog provides relief from summer heat and drought.

Seasonal foliage color
Spring Summer Fall Winter

Quercus deserticola (encino chaparro, encino del pedregal, encino texmole)

Family:
Fagaceae

Native range:
Central Mexico

This oak is a small single- or multitrunked tree growing to 6–8 m in height. Its small gray leaves are suggestive of the dry habitats in which it is found. New foliage emerges with a dense tomentum covering the bronze leaves to protect them from the sun.

Seasonal foliage color
Spring Summer Fall Winter

Robinia pseudoacacia (black locust)

Family:
Fabaceae

Native range:
Eastern United States

The black locust can grow to be 12–30 m tall and is typically found in young woodlands and disturbed areas. Being shade-intolerant, black locusts can quickly reforest open landscapes by sending out suckers. Loose drooping racemes of aromatic cream-white flowers hang from branches in the spring.

Seasonal foliage color
Spring Summer Fall Winter

Samanea saman (rain tree, umbrella tree, monkeypod, saman)

Family:
Fabaceae

Native range:
Central and South America

The saman is a wide-canopied tree that can grow 15–25 m tall. The large, symmetrical, umbrella-shaped crown creates beautiful shaded spaces below. The fine texture of the pinnate leaves is matched by the delicate pinkish flowers that can cover the entire tree when in full bloom.

Seasonal foliage color
Spring Summer Fall Winter

Schinus molle (Peruvian peppertree, aguaribay)

Family:
Anacardiaceae

Native range:
Peruvian Andes
to southern Brazil

The Peruvian peppertree is quick-growing, reaching heights of 15 m. Its rough grayish bark twists and flakes along the trunk, and the upper branches tend to become pendulous. The long pinnately compound leaves sway in the wind, giving this tree a gentle texture.

Seasonal foliage color
Spring Summer Fall Winter

Theobroma cacao (cacao)

Family:
Malvaceae

Native range:
Central America and
northwestern South America

The cacao tree grows to be 6–9 m tall in the humid and tropical climates of Central America, with glossy, oblong, drooping leaves. Its seeds are used to make cocoa, cocoa butter, and chocolate. Pink flowers are borne directly on the trunk and branches of the tree before giving way to long golden seedpods.

Seasonal foliage color
Spring Summer Fall Winter

Tipuana tipu (tipuana, tipa)

Family:
Fabaceae

Native range:
Southeastern South America

The tipuana tree can grow upwards of 30 m tall and has been naturalized in many parts of the world outside its native South American habitat. A flush of orange-yellow flowers erupts when it is in full bloom. The leaves are pinnately compound, with each leaflet being ovate, creating a dappled effect in the wide and spreading foliage.

Seasonal foliage color
Spring Summer Fall Winter

Triadica sebifera (Chinese tallow)

Family:
Euphorbiaceae

Native range:
Eastern China

Chinese tallow trees grow to 9–12 m tall and are native to China and Taiwan. The simple deciduous leaves are broad to ovate before ending in a pronounced peak at the tip. Leaves emerge bright green during the spring before giving way to a rush of yellows, oranges, purples, and reds in the autumn.

Seasonal foliage color
Spring Summer Fall Winter

Image Credits

Note: Sources are not cited for photographs and images by the authors, only for those by others and those used with permission.

Foreword

Fig. 1 © Ron Henderson

One Tree, Row, Two Trees, Allée, Grid, Hedge, Clump, Woods

Fig. 1 © Indianapolis Museum of Art; figs. 2–8 © Mohammad Arabmazar, April 2023

Increments of Time in Japanese Cherry Blossoms

Fig. 1 © Sano and Honda 1961; figs. 2A, 2B © Hans Friedl; fig. 5 © British Museum; fig. 6 © Minneapolis Institute of Art; fig. 7 © Art Institute of Chicago

Bursera simaruba

Figs. 3, 5 © Mauricio Ramos; fig. 4 Melville, Herman. 1935. *Typee: A Romance of the South Seas*. Introduction by Raymond Weaver and illustrations by Miguel Covarrubias, Illustrator. New York: Limited Editions Club.

Ceiba pentandra

Fig. 1 © Anwar Morales; fig. 3 © Michael Atwood, courtesy Indigenous Celebration; fig. 4A © CC BY-SA 4.0, Indies1, https://commons.wikimedia.org/wiki/User:Indies1; fig. 4B © Anwar Morales

Cupressus sempervirens

Figs. 3, 4 © Alamy; fig. 6 © Ron Henderson

Cyrtophyllum fragrans

Figs. 1, 2 © Louise Neo; fig. 3 © Teo Siyang; fig. 4 © National Archives of Singapore

Ficus macrophylla

Fig. 4 © Spackman Mossop Michaels

Liquidambar styraciflua

Fig. 1 © Reed Hilderbrand; fig. 4 © Richard Evans

Populus alba

Fig. 2 © Philadelphia Museum of Art

Populus nigra var. *italica*

Fig. 1 © Bibliothèque nationale de France; fig. 2 © Museo Histórico Nacional de Chile, Archivo Visual de Santiago; fig. 3 © Hume & Walker; fig. 4 © Montserrat Palmer; fig. 5 © Philippe Boisier

Robinia pseudoacacia

Figs. 1, 4–5 © Noventa Longo

Acknowledgments

> *It is already by* existing *that plants modify the world globally without even moving, without beginning to act. "To be" means, for them, to make world [faire monde]; reciprocally, to construct (our) world, to make world is only a synonym of "to be."*
>
> Emanuele Coccia, *The Life of Plants: A Metaphysics of Mixture*

Many family, friends, teachers, colleagues, and writers have inspired the lifetime love of trees that has culminated in this book: my granddad Harley, Patrick Hall, Esmée Bellalta, Anne Whiston Spirn, Charles Waldheim, Hu Jie, Tanya Kelley, Emanuele Coccia, Zhu Yufan, Richard Forman, Colin Franklin, Kim Mercurio, Michael Blier, Sue Weiler, Laura Solano, Stephen Stimson, Chandra Goldsmith Gray, Michelangelo Sabatino, Serge Ambrose, Jennifer Current, Nilay Mistry, Mark Jirik, Bruno Latour, Gina Crandell, Frank Balestri, Dorothée Imbert, Kathleen Emerson-Dell, Richard Olsen, Kurato Fujimoto, Fred Eychaner, Anne Hawley, Kyra Montagu, Trevor Lee, Doug Still, Jonathan Kavalier, Terry Harkness, Richard Powers, James Corner, Robert Pogue Harrison, Richard Polansky, Mike Tunkey, Andrew Bell, Arthur Takeuchi, Dick Roche, John Campanini, Barbara Sokoloff, Julian Bonder, John Beardsley, Frank Flury, Takayuki Tanaka, Sonja Dümpelmann, Kibo Hagino, Yuki Hagino, Tim Baird, Paul Haddad, Art Johnson, Dan Rose, Frank Montana, Colgate Searle, Lilly Dick, Fabrizio Gallante, Jim Heroux, George and Yara Cadwalader, Gareth Doherty, Einar Jarmund, Glenn Murcutt, Alfred Caldwell, Sano Toemon, Chisao Shigemori, Cindy Sanders, Maria Debye Saxinger, Dennis McGlade, Victoria Steiger, Heidi Shusterman, Ian McHarg, and all the insightful contributors to this compendium of trees. **Tree people are good people.**

Illinois Institute of Technology Landscape Architecture + Urbanism Program graduate assistants Valerie Clarke and Tao "Tammy" Xu organized initial drafts of the nascent book. Hans Friedl maintained the orderliness of the final manuscript and images, and he drew the leaf portraits that populate the book.

Patrick Hubenthal's proofreading expertise elegantly blended regional languages about trees into the text, and Floyd E. Schulze designed a lively book as richly layered as scattered leaves on the ground. David Marold, Katharina Holas, and everyone at Birkhäuser have supported this project with enthusiasm and wisdom—and allowed us to add extra words about trees. All the contributors had much to say, so thank you for letting the book, like the trees, have space to grow.

Ron Henderson (Ed.)
Professor of Landscape Architecture + Urbanism,
Illinois Institute of Technology
Founding Principal, LIRIO Landscape Architecture

Concept:
Ron Henderson and Gary Hilderbrand

Acquisitions Editor:
David Marold, Birkhäuser Verlag, Vienna, Austria

Content and Production Editor:
Katharina Holas, Birkhäuser Verlag, Vienna, Austria

Proofreading:
Patrick Hubenthal, Albuquerque, USA

Layout, cover design, and typography:
Floyd E. Schulze, Birkhäuser Verlag, Berlin, Germany

Image editing:
Pixelstorm Litho & Digital Imaging, Vienna, Austria

Printing:
Beltz Grafische Betriebe GmbH, Bad Langensalza, Germany

Paper:
Magno Natural 120 gsm

Typeface:
Söhne by Kris Sowersby

Library of Congress Control Number: 2023935982

Bibliographic information published by the German National Library
The German National Library lists this publication in the Deutsche Nationalbibliografie;
detailed bibliographic data are available on the Internet at http://dnb.dnb.de.

ISBN 978-3-0356-2731-2
e-ISBN (PDF) 978-3-0356-2732-9

MIX
Papier | Fördert
gute Waldnutzung
FSC® C089473

Im Westfeld 8, 4055 Basel, Switzerland
Part of Walter de Gruyter GmbH, Berlin/Boston

9 8 7 6 5 4 3 2 1

www.birkhauser.com